8th GRADE TECHNOLOGY

A COMPREHENSIVE CURRICULUM

SIXTH EDITION

Part Nine of the SL Technology Curriculum

Version 6.3 2021

Visit the companion website at Ask a Tech Teacher for more resources to teach technology

ISBN 978-1-942101-30-7

Printed in the United States of America

Introduction

The educational paradigm has changed—again. Technology has become granular to learning, blended into educational standards from Kindergarten on, like these that expect students to:

- demonstrate sufficient command of **keyboarding** to type at least three pages in a single sitting
- **evaluate different media** [print or digital]
- **gather information** from print/digital sources
- integrate and evaluate **information presented in diverse media** and formats
- **interpret information** presented visually, orally, or quantitatively [such as interactive Web pages]
- make **strategic use of digital media**
- use **print/digital glossaries/dictionaries** ...
- use information from **images and words in print/digital** text
- communicate with a **variety of media**
- **use text features and search tools** (e.g., key words, sidebars, **hyperlinks**) to locate information

But how is this taught?

With the nine-volume **Structured Learning Technology Curriculum**. Aligned with Common Core Standards* and National Educational Technology Standards, and using a time-proven method honed in classrooms, students learn the technology that promotes literacy,

critical thinking, problem-solving, and decision-making through project-based work. The purpose is not to teach step-by-step tech skills (like adding borders, formatting a document, and creating a blog). There are many fine books for that. What this curriculum does is guide you in providing the **right skills at the right time**.

Just as most children can't learn to read at two, or write at four, they shouldn't be required to place hands on home row in kindergarten or use the Internet before they understand the digital risks and responsibilities. The Structured Learning curriculum makes sure students get what they need at the right age with proper scaffolding. The end result is a phenomenal amount of learning in a short period of time.

For skills you don't know, visit our Help blog, AskATechTeacher. There's always someone there who can help.

"New technologies have broadened and expanded the role that speaking and listening play in acquiring and sharing knowledge and have tightened their link to other forms of communication. Digital texts confront students with the potential for continually updated content and dynamically changing combinations of words, graphics, images, hyperlinks, and embedded video and audio."

—CCSS

"Use of technology differentiates for student learning styles by providing an alternative method of achieving conceptual understanding, procedural skill and fluency, and applying this knowledge to authentic circumstances."

—CCSS

What's in the SL Technology Curriculum?

The SL Curriculum is project-based and collaborative with wide-ranging opportunities for students to show their knowledge in the manner that fits their communication and learning style. Each grade level includes topics to be woven into 'most' 21st-century lesson plans:

- *keyboarding—more than typing*
- *digital citizenship—critical with the influx of Chromebooks and iPads*
- *problem-solving—to encourage independence, critical thinking*
- *vocabulary—decode unknown words in any subject quickly*

For more on this, read *"4 Things Every Teacher Must Teach and How"* at the end of Lesson 1.

Besides these four topics, here's a quick overview of what is included in the curriculum:

- *curated list of assessments and images*
- *articles that address tech pedagogy*
- *Certificate of Completion for students*
- *curriculum map of skills taught*
- *monthly homework (3rd-8th only)*
- *posters to visually represent topics*
- *Scope and Sequence of skills taught*
- *step-by-step weekly lessons*

Each weekly lesson includes:

- *assessment strategies*
- *class warm-up and exit ticket*
- *Common Core and ISTE Standards*
- *differentiation strategies*
- *educational applications*
- *essential question and big idea*
- *examples, rubrics, images, printables*
- *homework (for students)*
- *materials/preparation required*
- *problem solving for lesson*
- *steps to accomplish goals*
- *time required to complete*
- *vocabulary used*

Figure 1a-b shows the lesson detail that can be found at the beginning and the end of each curricular lesson:

Figure 1a-b—What's included in each lesson

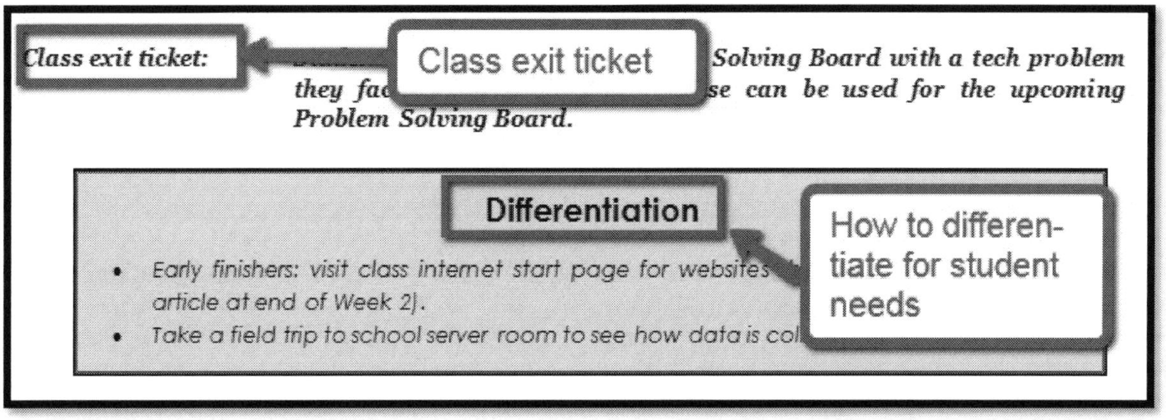

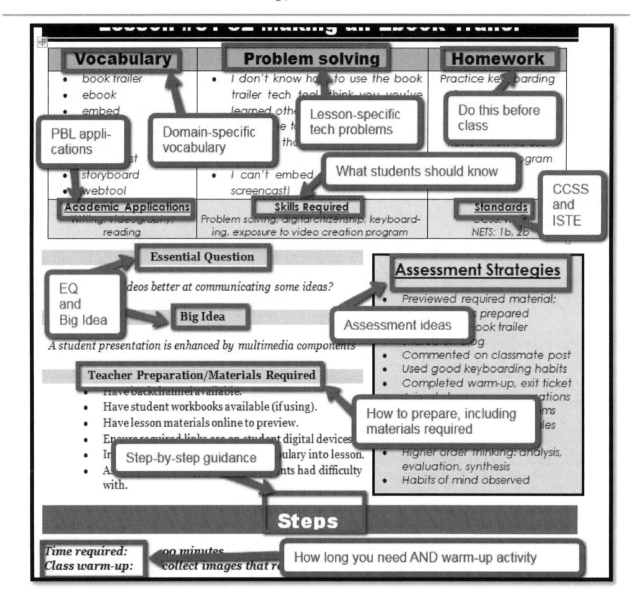

What's New in the Sixth Edition?

A good tech curriculum is aligned with best practices, which means frequent updates. Consider these changes in the Sixth Edition:

- *Lessons are now as likely to be used by any member of the **grade-level team**. You'll learn how to unpack the lesson regardless of which hat you wear.*
- *Ideas are provided to deliver lessons on all **popular digital**.*
- *The importance of **higher order thinking**— analysis, evaluation and synthesis—is called out.*
- *The importance of '**habits of mind'**—critical to college and career goals—is included.*
- ***Differentiation** is encouraged. Teachers learn strategies to meet students where they learn.*
- *Each lesson includes a **warm-up and exit ticket**, to assess and reinforce student learning.*
- *Each grade-level curriculum includes **student workbooks** (sold separately).*

Who Needs This Book

You are the Tech Specialist, Coordinator for Instructional Technology, IT Coordinator, Technology Facilitator or Director, Curriculum Specialist, or tech teacher—tasked with finding the right project for a classroom. You have a limited budget, less software, and the drive to do it right no matter roadblocks.

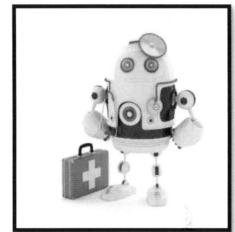

Or you are a grade-level teacher, a tech enthusiast with a goal this year—and this time you mean it—to integrate the wonders of technology into lessons. You've seen it work. Others in your PLN are doing it. And significantly, you want to comply with state/national requirements and/or IB guidelines that weave technology into the fabric of inquiry.

You are a homeschooler. Even though you're not comfortable with technology, you know your children must be. You are committed to providing the tools s/he needs to succeed. Just as important: Your child WANTS to learn with these tools!

How do you reach your goal? With this curriculum. Teaching children to strategically and safely use technology is a vital part of being a functional member of society—and should be part of every curriculum. If not you (the teacher), who will do this? To build **Tomorrow's Student** (*Figure 2*) requires integration of technology and learning. We show you how.

Figure 2—Tomorrow's student

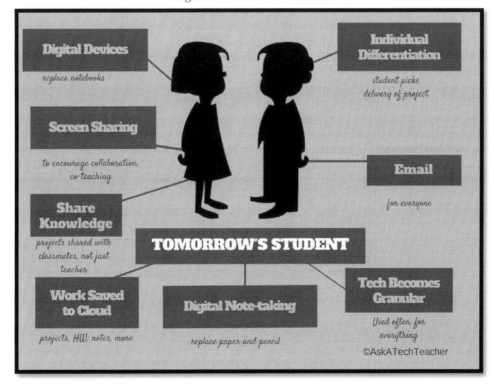

How to Use This Book

You can use this curriculum on its own—as a teacher manual—or in conjunction with the companion student workbooks (sold separately through Structured Learning LLC). Either way, contact Zeke at admin@structuredlearning.net for free start-up training.

If there is a skill students don't get, circle back on it, especially when you see it come up a second or third time through the course of the K-8 curricula. By the end of 8th grade, students have a well-rounded tech toolkit that serves their learning needs and prepares them for college and/or career.

The curriculum map (*Figure 3*) shows what's covered in which grade. Units taught multiple years reflect increasingly less scaffolding and more student direction. Here's how to use it:

- Determine what skills were covered earlier years. Expect students to transfer that knowledge to this new school year. Review the topics and skills, but don't expect to teach.
- For skills covered prior years, confirm that was done. If not (for whatever reason), when you reach lessons that require the skills, plan extra time.

Figure 3—Curriculum Map—K-8

	Mouse Skills	Vocabulary - Hardware	Problem-solving	Platform	Keyboard	WP	Slide-shows	DTP	Spread-sheet	Google Earth	Search/ Research	Graphics/	Co-ding	WWW	Games	Dig Cit
K	☺	☺	☺	☺	☺					☺		☺	☺	☺		☺
1	☺	☺	☺	☺	☺	☺	☺	☺	☺	☺		☺	☺	☺		☺
2		☺	☺	☺	☺	☺	☺	☺	☺	☺		☺	☺	☺		☺
3		☺	☺	☺	☺	☺	☺	☺	☺	☺	☺	☺	☺	☺		☺
4		☺	☺		☺	☺	☺	☺	☺	☺	☺	☺	☺	☺	☺	☺
5		☺	☺		☺	☺		☺	☺	☺	☺	☺	☺	☺		☺
6		☺	☺	☺	☺	☺	☺	☺	☺	☺	☺	☺	☺	☺		☺
7		☺	☺	☺	☺				☺	☺	☺	☺	☺	☺	☺	☺
8		☺	☺	☺	☺	☺			☺	☺	☺	☺	☺	☺	☺	☺

Here are hints on using this curriculum:

- This curriculum optionally uses the 'flipped classroom' approach. Homework prepares students for the class lesson so class time is spent on enrichment. Homework can be shared via the class website, blog, or LMS.
- A number of lessons are mixed throughout the year:

  Digital Citizenship
  Keyboarding
  Problem Solving

- 'Academic Applications' provide suggestions on how to blend lessons into your curriculum.

- Invest in student digital workbooks (sold separately through Structured Learning LLC), a student-centric companion to the teacher guide. Here are several reasons why:

  Figure 1--Student workbook

  - *Full-color projects with directions are at student fingertips (licensing varies by plan).*
  - *Workbooks can be viewed and annotated.*
  - *Students can work at their own pace.*

- Most lessons start with a warm-up to get students into tech and you to finish a prior class.
- 'Teacher Preparation' often includes chatting with the grade-level team so you can *tie tech into their inquiry.*
- Some lessons offer several activities to meet goals of the Essential Question and Big Idea. Pick what works best for your group.
- Check off completed items on the line preceding the step so you know what to get back to when you have time. If you have the ebook, use an annotation tool that works for your devices.

- *indicates video*

- *indicates work with a partner*

- *indicates an article*

- *indicates a poster (in Appendix)*

- *indicates workbook material*

- Use as much technology as possible in your classroom. Make it adaptive and native whether it's a smartphone timing a quiz, a video of activities posted to the class website, or an audio file with student input. If you treat tech as a tool in daily activities, so will students.
- Encourage student-directed differentiation. If the Big Idea and Essential Question can be accommodated in other ways, embrace those.
- If you have the digital book, zoom in on posters, rubrics, lessons to enlarge as needed.
- Organically use lesson vocabulary. Students gain authentic understanding by your example.
- Expect students to direct their own learning. You are a 'guide on the side', a facilitator not lecturer. Learning is accomplished by both success and failure.
- Expect students to be risk takers. Don't rush to solve their problems. Ask them to think how it was done in the past. Focus on problems listed in the lesson but embrace all that come your way. **This scaffolds critical thinking when you won't be there to help.**

- Lessons expect students to develop 'habits of mind' (*Figure 5*). Read more about Art Costa and Bena Kallick's discussion of these principles in the article at the end of Lesson #1. In a sentence: Habits of Mind ask students to engage in learning, not simply memorize.

Figure 5—Habits of Mind

- Don't expect free time while students work. Move among them to provide assistance and observations on their keyboarding, problem-solving, and vocabulary decoding skills.
- Every effort has been made to accommodate all digital devices. Lesson samples are often in multiple platforms. If the activity is impossible on your digital device (i.e., iPads don't have mouses; software doesn't run in Chromebooks), focus on the **Big Idea and Essential Question**—the skill taught and its application to inquiry. Adapt instructions as you follow steps.

More Help

Need more help? Visit the companion website, Ask a Tech Teacher©, run by teachers using the curriculum. Here, you'll find:

- *free lesson plans*
- *targeted websites*
- *free tech tips and weekly newsletters*
- *free training videos on tools used in lesson plans*
- *great apps to include on iPads, digital devices*
- *lots of links*

And more. You can also email admin@structuredlearning.net or askatechteacher@gmail.com.

Finally, here are useful pieces to extend this curriculum:

- *Student workbooks—(sold separately by Structured Learning) allow students to be self-paced*
- *Digital Citizenship curriculum (sold separately by SL)— if this is a school focus (sold separately)*
- *Keyboarding Curriculum (sold separately by SL)— if this is a school focus (sold separately)*

Copyrights

About the Authors

Ask a Tech Teacher is a group of technology teachers who run an award-winning resource blog. Here they provide free materials, advice, lesson plans, pedagogical conversation, website reviews, and more to all who drop by. The free newsletters and articles help thousands of teachers, homeschoolers, and those serious about finding the best way to maneuver the minefields of technology in education.

*Throughout this text, we refer to Common Core State Standards and a license granted to "...copy, publish, distribute, and display the Common Core State Standards for purposes that support the CCSS Initiative. Copyright 2010. National Governors Association Center for Best Practices and Council of Chief State School Officers. All rights reserved.

Table of Contents

Scope and Sequence

Lessons

Arranged by theme

Basics

Logical Thinking

Digital Citizenship

Search/Research

Programming

Collaborate/Publish/Present

Articles

Appendix

Posters

Certificates

Table of Images

Table of Assessments

GRADE 6-8 TECH SCOPE AND SEQUENCE©

Aligned with ISTE (International Society for Technology in Education) and Common Core State Standards
Check each skill off with I (Introduced), W (Working on), or M (Mastered)
Organized by ISTE Standards 1-7

	Empowered Learner	6	7	8
	Use technology and digital media strategically and capably (CCSS C&CR profile)	W	M	M
	Are familiar with the strengths and limitations of various technological tools and mediums and can select and use those best suited to communication goals (CCSS C&CR Profile)	W	M	M
	Strategize personal learning			
	Understand how inquiry contributes to creative and empowered learning	W	W	M
	Understand how technology contributes to classroom and personal learning	W	M	M
	Understand how higher order thinking skills are buttressed by technology	W	M	M
	Select between available options, choosing one best suited to learning	W	M	M
	Compare-contrast available tools, determining which is best suited to need	W	M	M
	Know what digital tools are available and how to use them (i.e., blogs, annotation)	M	M	M
	Be responsive to varied needs of task-audience-purpose	M	M	M
	Interact, collaborate, publish with peers employing a variety of digital media	W	M	M
	Develop cultural understanding by engaging with learners of other cultures	W	M	M
	Seek feedback to demonstrate learning			
	Add comments to class blogs, forums, discussion boards, webtools	M	M	M
	Work in groups collaboratively and productively	M	M	M
	Transfer knowledge			
	Scaffold learning year-to-year and lesson-to-lesson	M	M	M
	Transfer understanding of one digital tool or device to others	M	M	M
	Use familiar tech tools (like Google Earth's ruler) to solve real-world problems	M	M	M
	Hardware			
	Know parts of digital devices and how to connect them	M	M	M
	Can troubleshoot hardware	M	M	M
	Operating Systems (PC, Mac, Chromebook, iPads)			
	Know how to find files, add more, and save to network file folder and/or cloud	M	M	M
	Know how to drag-drop (or copy-paste) within a doc and between folders	M	M	M
	Know how to use tool tips (hover over icon) and right-click menus	M	M	M
	Can troubleshoot operating systems	M	M	M
	Online Tech for Classroom Management			
	Understand school technology	W	M	M
	Understand Cloud for transferring school work to home	M	M	M
	Know how to annotate a PDF or online document	W	M	M
	Know how to share out classwork (including homework)	I	W	M
	Know how to use online vocabulary decoding tools quickly and efficiently	M	M	M

Keyboarding			
Know how to practice keyboarding on internet sites and software	M	M	M
Strive to achieve grade-appropriate keyboarding speed and accuracy goal	M	M	M
Practice touch typing	M	M	M
Compose at keyboard by creating classroom-based projects	M	M	M
Understand speed difference between handwriting and keyboarding	M	M	M
Select shortkeys instead of toolbar tools when appropriate	M	M	M
Use correct posture, elbows at sides	M	M	M
Know parts of keyboard--keys, numbers, F keys, arrows, Esc	W	M	M
Word Processing			
Know when to use a word processing program, both software and online tools	W	M	M
Use classroom principles of grammar, spelling when word processing on computer	M	M	M
Know basic page layout--heading, title, body, footer	W	M	M
Know how to use the thesaurus	M	M	M
Know how to format a document—i.e., header, footer, border, cover page, embedded link	W	M	M
Can troubleshoot word processing	W	M	M
Google Earth			
Display familiarity with tools for moving around world	M	M	M
Run a tour of placemarks around the planet	W	M	M
2 Digital Citizen			
Gather relevant information from print and digital sources, assess credibility, and integrate the information while avoiding plagiarism. (CCSS C&CR Writing Anchor Standards)	I	W	M
Internet privacy and safety			
Know how to configure privacy settings	I	W	M
Understand cyberbullying, use of passwords	M	M	M
Understand digital footprint and online presence	I	W	M
Understand how online entities track student activity online	I	W	M
Understand the appropriate use of the 'digital neighborhood'	M	M	M
Legal use of online materials			
Discuss copyright law, fair use, intellectual property, rights and obligations of digital world	W	M	M
Discuss plagiarism and how to cite sources	W	M	M
Digital Netiquette			
Understand etiquette in the digital neighborhood	M	M	M
Digital Citizenship			
Understand what a 'digital citizen' is	M	M	M
Exhibit a positive attitude toward technology that supports collaboration and learning	M	M	M
Demonstrate personal responsibility for lifelong learning	M	M	M
Exhibit leadership for digital citizenship--set the standard for classmates	M	M	M
Interactions online			
Address digital commerce	I	W	M
Use safe, responsible and ethical behavior on the internet	M	M	M
Discuss social media	I	W	M

		Discuss digital rights and responsibilities	M	M	M
		Recognize irresponsible and unsafe practices on the internet	I	W	M
		Know how online comments follow same rules as speaking and listening	I	W	M
3	**Knowledge Constructor**				
		Use the internet to build strong content knowledge (CCSS C&CR profile)	M	M	M
		Use technology to produce and publish writing and collaborate with others (CCRA.W.6)	M	M	M
		Use technology and digital media strategically and capably (CCSS C&CR profile)	M	M	M
		Comprehend as well as critique. (CCSS C&CR profile)	W	M	M
		Value evidence (CCSS C&CR profile)	W	M	M
		Compare-contrast documents across varied digital media (CCSS Anchor Standards)	W	M	M
		Gather relevant information from multiple digital sources (CCRA.W.8)	W	M	M
		Assess credibility of digital sources used for research (CCSS Anchor Standards)	W	M	M
		Integrate and evaluate information from diverse media (CCRA.R.7)	W	M	M
		Make strategic use of digital media to express information (CCRA.SL.5)	W	M	M
		Use electronic menus and links to locate key facts (RI/)	W	M	M
	Effective online research strategies				
		Use screenshots to collect information	W	M	M
		Locate, organize, analyze, evaluate, and synthesize information from a variety of sources	M	M	M
		Evaluate and select information sources and digital tools based on task	W	M	M
		Know how to search effectively and efficiently, limit search as needed, and use Ctrl+F	I	W	M
		Know how to effectively use LMS systems and the Cloud	I	W	M
	Technology as knowledge curator				
		Evaluate the accuracy, perspective, relevancy of information, media, data	I	W	M
		Curate information from digital resources using a variety of tools and methods that demonstrate meaningful connections or conclusions (such as outlines, mindmaps).	I	W	M
		Present information in a manner suited to task, audience, and purpose (i.e., infographics, graphic organizers, Google Earth)	M	M	M
		Build knowledge by exploring real-world issues, developing ideas, and pursuing solutions using online learning programs	M	M	M
	Online collaborative environments				
		Use blogs for journaling and tracking project progress	W	M	M
		Incorporate text, images, widgets to better communicate ideas	W	M	M
		Know how to use Discussion boards and forums	I	W	M
4	**Innovative Designer**				
		Respond to varying demands of audience, task, purpose, discipline (CCSS C&CR profile)	M	M	M
		Use glossaries or dictionaries to clarify meaning of key words and phrases (CCSS.L.K.4)	M	M	M
		Gather, comprehend, evaluate, synthesize, and report on information in order to answer questions or solve problems, (CCSS Key Design Consideration)	W	M	M
		Draw on information from multiple print or digital sources, demonstrating the ability to locate an answer to a question quickly or to solve a problem efficiently (CCSS. RI.5)	I	W	M
		Reason abstractly and quantitatively (CCSS. Math.Practice.MP2)	M	M	M
		Use appropriate tools strategically (CCSS. Math.Practice.MP5)	M	M	M
		Attend to precision (CCSS. Math.Practice.MP6)	M	M	M
	Design Process				

Use planning tools such as mindmaps to organize ideas and solve problems	I	W	M
Use presentation tools like screencasts, videos, and trailers to share in-depth topical ideas and solve authentic problems in a variety of creative ways	I	W	M
Use templates and patterns to create new designs (like shapes, letters)	M	M	M
Select and use digital tools (such as comics) to plan and manage a design process that considers design constraints and calculated risk	M	M	M
Develop, test and refine prototypes as part of a cyclical design process	W	M	M
Able to tolerate ambiguity, persevere, with a capacity to work with open-ended problems.	M	M	M
Use established patterns and design processes in solving common tech problems	M	M	M
Recognize the part 'failure' plays in solving problems	M	M	M

Decision Making

Identify and define authentic problems and questions for investigation	M	M	M
Collect, analyze data to identify solutions and make informed decisions	M	M	M
Able to debug programs using sequencing, if-then thinking, logic, or other strategies	M	M	M
Able to evaluate which program is right for which task	M	M	M

Slideshows

Know when and how to use presentation tools as software and online tools	W	M	M
Understand how to deliver a professional presentation	W	M	M
Can troubleshoot presentation tools	M	M	M

Graphics

Use drawing software and web-based tools efficiently	M	M	M
Know how to create and annotate screenshots to share information	M	M	M

Desktop publishing

Can identify parts of the desktop publishing screen	W	M	M
Know when to use a desktop publishing program to share information	W	M	M
Know how to plan a publication	I	W	M
Can troubleshoot publishing tools	W	M	M

Screencasts, Videos

Know how to create screencasts, videos, and trailers to share information	I	W	M
Know how to upload screencasts , videos, trailers to easily-accessible locations for peers	I	W	M
Know how to use the design process to prepare screencasts	I	W	M

5 Computational Thinker

Gather, evaluate, synthesize, and report on information to conduct original research in order to answer questions or solve problems, (CCSS Key Design Consideration)	M	M	M
Draw on information from multiple sources, demonstrating the ability to locate an answer to a question quickly or to solve a problem efficiently (CCSS. RI.5)	M	M	M
Make sense of problems and persevere in solving them (CCSS. Math.Practice.MP1)	M	M	M
Reason abstractly and quantitatively (CCSS. Math.Practice.MP2)	M	M	M
Construct viable arguments and critique the reasoning of others (CCSS. Math.Practice.MP3)	M	M	M
Model with mathematics (CCSS. Math.Practice.MP4)	M	M	M
Use appropriate tools strategically (CCSS. Math.Practice.MP5)	M	M	M
Attend to precision (CCSS. Math.Practice.MP6)	M	M	M

		Look for and make use of structure (CCSS. Math.Practice.MP7)	M	M	M
		Look for and express regularity in repeated reasoning (CCSS. Math.Practice.MP8)	M	M	M
	Critical Thinking				
		Understand how to identify, define authentic problems, questions	M	M	M
		Know how to use digital tools available including blogs, websites, annotation tools	M	M	M
		Always attempt to solve a problem before asking for teacher assistance	M	M	M
		Know how to research and develop an argument to present (such as for a debate)	I	W	M
		Know how to use programs not yet learned	M	M	M
		Know why a particular digital tool is suited to a specific need	M	M	M
		Know how to analyze data digitally to facilitate problem-solving and decision-making.	I	W	M
	Problem solving				
		Identify, define, and solve authentic problems, questions for investigation	M	M	M
		Know how to access work from anywhere in the school	M	M	M
		Know how to solve common hardware problems	M	M	M
		Know what to do if computer doesn't work	I	W	M
		Can trouble shoot a non-working program	I	W	M
		Can break problems into component parts, extract key information, and develop descriptive models to understand complex systems or facilitate problem-solving.	I	W	W
	Programming				
		Understand technology contributes to higher-order thinking, DoK, or another	W	M	M
		Understand the cause-effect relationship inherent in actions	W	M	M
		Eagerly experiment with programming tools	M	M	M
		Understand how automation works; use algorithmic thinking to develop a sequence of steps to create and test automated solutions. (i.e., timelines, brainstorming)	W	W	W
		Able to debug programs using sequencing, if-then thinking, logic, or other strategies	W	W	W
	Robotics				
		Contribute to project teams to produce original works or solve problems		I	W
		Build, program, debug a robot		I	W
		Trouble shoot simple problems		I	W
		Use sensors to monitor the environment and able to measure distances with robots		I	W
	Spreadsheets				
		Process and sort data, report results by collecting data and reporting it	I	W	M
		Know how to publish spreadsheet through a widget to blog and/or website	I	W	M
		Can troubleshoot spreadsheets	I	W	W
6	**Creative Communicator**				
		Use technology and digital media strategically and capably (CCSS C&CR profile)	W	M	M
		Use technology to produce and publish writing and collaborate with others (ELA-LITERACY.CCRA.W.6)	M	M	M
		Explore digital tools to produce and publish writing (CCSS.ELA-Literacy.W)	M	M	M
		Explore digital tools to collaborate with peers (CCSS.ELA-Literacy.W)	M	M	M
		Use multimedia to aid comprehension (CCSS.ELA-Literacy.W)	W	M	M
		Ask and answer questions from information presented (CCSS.ELA-Literacy.SL)	M	M	M

		Include audio recordings and multimedia to enhance main ideas (CCSS.ELA-Literacy.SL)	W	M	M
		Integrate and evaluate information presented in diverse media and formats, including visually, quantitatively, and orally (CCSS.ELA-LITERACY.CCRA.SL.2)	M	M	M
		Use multimedia to organize ideas, concepts, info (CCSS.ELA-Literacy.WHST)	M	M	M
	Blogs				
		Interact, collaborate, publish with peers employing a variety of digital media	W	M	M
		Develop cultural understanding and global awareness by engaging other cultures	W	M	M
	Digital Tools				
		Communicate information, ideas to multiple audiences using a variety of media and formats including visual organizers, comics, Twitter (where appropriate), and more	W	M	M
		Use web-based communication tools to share unique and individual ideas	W	M	M
		Learn a variety of tools that address varied communication styles (from written to visual to video) by teaching them to classmates	W	M	M
		Know how to use models and simulations to explore complex systems and issues	W	M	M
		Develop cultural understanding by engaging with learners of other cultures	M	M	M
	Digital Storytelling, Debate				
		Work collaboratively to develop a persuasive argument (such as for a debate)	M	M	M
		Participate in a virtual field trip that tells the story of a student's experience	M	M	M
	Speaking and Listening				
		Engage in impromptu speaking such as the Evidence Board	I	W	W
		Present well-prepared presentations knowing how to use multimedia props	W	M	M
		Engage in short presentations such as the Presentation Boards	I	W	M
		Interact, collaborate, and publish with peers or others employing a variety of digital media	W	M	M
7	**Global Collaborator**				
		Understand other perspectives and cultures. (CCSS C&CR profile)	M	M	M
		Respond to demands of audience, task, purpose, discipline. (CCSS C&CR Profile)	M	M	M
		Use digital tools to connect with learners from a variety of backgrounds and cultures, engaging with them in ways that broaden mutual understanding and learning	M	M	M
		Explore local and global issues and use collaborative technologies to investigate solutions	M	M	M
	Collaborate with Others				
		Use collaborative technologies to work with others, including peers, experts or community members, to examine issues and problems from multiple viewpoints.	I	W	M
		Contribute constructively to project teams to work effectively toward a common goal.	I	W	M
		Use blogs, forums, Discussion Boards to collaborate and share	I	W	M
		Work in groups to teach technology skills to others	I	W	M

Lesson #1 Introduction

Vocabulary	Problem solving	Homework
• Back-up • Digital • Digital citizen • Right-click menu • Save-as • Save early/often • Select-do • Technology • Webtool	• What's the difference between 'save' and 'save-as'? • What's a quick way to ** (shortkey)? • How do I annotate student workbook (check Digital Tools Lesson)? • I don't have a flash drive (how do you back up files?) • I can't do my keyboarding homework at home (come to afterschool club)	What class rules would you add? What is a 'flipped classroom'? What's 'tech'? Review teacher-provided materials
Academic Applications *problem solving, critical thinking*	**Required skills** *knowledge of keyboarding, tech problem solving, and digital devices; comfort with tech*	**Standards** *CCSS: Anchor Standards NETS: 1a, 1b*

Essential Question

How do I use technology to share with classmates?

Big Idea

Students use tech to enhance their education

Teacher Preparation/Materials Required

- Have student workbooks available (if using).
- Have a list of class rules from last year.
- Have Exit Ticket class poll ready.
- Have class syllabus (or use text table of contents).
- Ensure required links are on student digital devices.
- Integrate domain-specific tech vocabulary into lesson.
- Know whether you need extra time to complete the lesson.
- Have info on afterschool Keyboard Club and Help time.
- Something happen you weren't prepared for? No worries. Show students how you fix the emergency without a meltdown and with a positive attitude.

Assessment Strategies

- *Previewed required material; came to class prepared*
- *Annotated workbook (if using)*
- *Completed exit ticket*
- *Joined classroom conversations*
- *[tried to] solve own problems*
- *Decisions followed class rules*
- *Left room as s/he found it*
- *Higher order thinking: analysis, evaluation, synthesis*
- *Habits of mind observed*

Steps

Time required: **45 minutes**
Class warm-up: **None**

_____ **Homework for lesson is assigned early so students are prepared.**

_____ Tour classroom to familiarize students with the tech devices that will assist them this year. Printer? Class announcements? Evidence Board? What else?

_____ What does 'technology' mean at your school? Do students understand 'tech in education'? How have they used it? Is *Figure 6a* or *Figure 6b* more accurate in their minds?

Figure 6a-b—Which image represents 'technology'?

_____Success in 8th-grade tech is predicated on student enthusiasm for learning, transfer of knowledge, and evidence of critical thinking skills. Students will often 'pick which program works best' or 'devise a plan to accomplish goals' or 'teach themselves'.

_____Discuss student tech background, what they know and want to know, and difficulties they see taking this class. Discuss your expectations.

_____Understand domain-specific technology language pursued two ways:

- *Students use correct 'geek' words during class, as do you. Tech words students don't know will be added to a virtual wall or a similar collection spot.*
- *Every time students find a word they don't understand, decode it—use the class dictionary tool, ask friends, or ask the teacher. Don't skip over it.*

_____Discuss the focus of 8th grade technology:

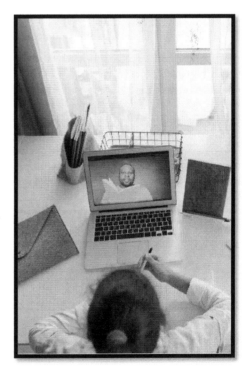

1. Think critically:

- *Determine which program, tools and strategies work best for what activity*
- *devise solutions to problems based on past knowledge*
- *trouble-shoot; find alternatives*
- *work collaboratively to draw on everyone's knowledge*
- *understand what you do and don't know, and the difference*
- *research answers effectively, efficiently, and ethically*

2. Employ problem-solving skills:

- *use available tools to solve a problem*
- *critically think about a problem; ignore chaff; focus on pertinent details*
- *present information so others understand*
- *make sense of data*

3. **Transfer knowledge:**

- *...to other parts of academic and social life*
- *publish and share online to collaborate and seek constructive criticism*
- *create a digital portfolio accessible from many locations*
- *link information to others*

4. **Be a good digital citizenship:**

- *learn to thrive in the digital world*
- *learn fundamentals of research, social media, and communication*
- *understand rights and responsibilities of those in the digital world*

5. **Learn fundamental tech skills:**

- *learn to type faster than you think*
- *know how to word process in many programs*
- *turn data into information*
- *make presentations effective, responsive to the audience, and interesting*
- *understand tech hardware and how to troubleshoot when needed*
- *understand digital devices needed to thrive in the learning community*
- *know online tools and what they can be used for*

Review class syllabus and goals. Use this text's Table of Contents and Scope and Sequence if desired. This year, class is less about tech skills and more about higher order thinking. Briefly review each theme in the Table of Contents. 'Sell" it as exciting and useful:

- **Basics**—*Why is keyboarding important? Why is understanding tech important? How can understanding hardware help students use tech efficiently and with fewer problems? How does selecting the right tool affect communication?*
- **Digital citizenship**—*How can students thrive in the virtual neighborhood? What are the rights and responsibilities they must consider?*
- **Search and Research**—*How can*

students use the boundless resources of the internet effectively, efficiently, legally?

- **Programming**—*How does coding teach critical thinking and problem solving? How can robotics, programming and SketchUp make those lessons fun and easy?*
- **Logical thinking**—*How can technology teach critical thinking? How can bridge building, visual learning, robotics, Scratch, and programming show how to recognize/solve problems?*
- **Collaborate/Publish/Present**—*How can students share their knowledge with classmates and the world?*

_____Collect class rules from students that will make class productive, efficient, and fair for all students. They might include (see *Figure 7* and full-size sample at end of lesson):

- *Save early, save often, about every ten minutes.*
- *No food or drink around digital devices.*
- *Respect the work of others and yourself.*
- *Keep your body to yourself—don't touch neighbor's digital device.*
- *No excuses; don't blame people or computer.*
- *Help neighbor with words, not by doing.*
- *When collaborating, build on others' ideas as you clearly express your own.*
- *As a general rule: Select first, then do. You can't do the latter without the former.*

Figure 7—Class rules

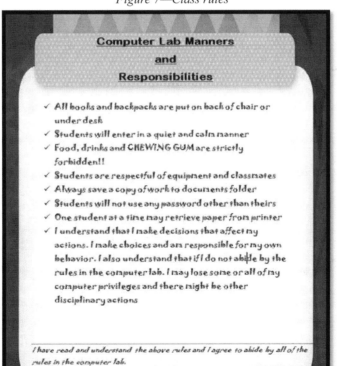

_____If using workbooks, students handwrite suggested rules into the PDF.
_____Discuss class warm-ups and exit tickets (see **article at end of this lesson**).

_____Students will learn to be good digital citizens (see *Digital Citizenship*).

_____Students will learn to use a wide range of web tools (see *Digital Tools*) in class.

_____Let students know that you are open to alternative suggestions on tools to use for class projects. For example, if you suggest Wordle, a student can request Tagxedo. Expect them to use **evidence** to build their case, **compare-contrast** their tool to your suggestions, and **draw logical conclusions**. Approve the change if the tool fulfills guidelines.

_____Offer an after school **Keyboarding Club** two days a week for students who can't do their homework at home. Limit it to 45 minutes.

_____Offer **after-school help** on Keyboarding Club days for those who need assistance with tech or a project involving tech. Request student volunteers to assist. Collaborate with your school's STAR program, where volunteering is part of class requirements.

_____This class is 'flipped'. Briefly: Students prepare for the class with videos, articles, research, text—whatever prepares them for class activities. It will not take longer than normal homework but will be used in class the next day to complete activities. Post *Figure 8* (poster in Appendix) somewhere in your classroom as a reminder:

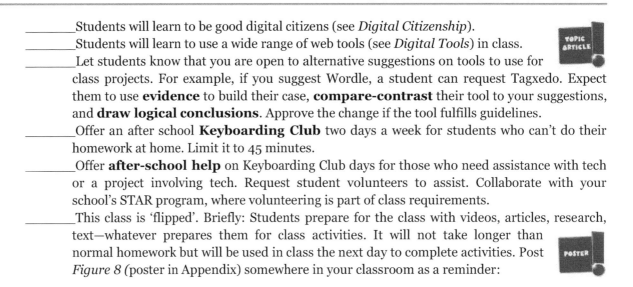

Figure 8—Flipped classroom

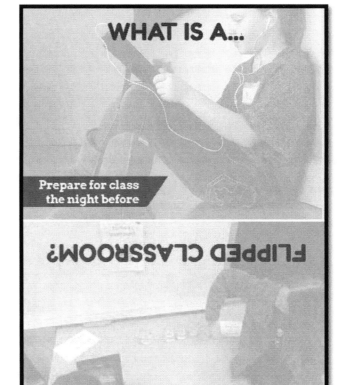

_____Discuss this approach as a group until it is clear. Point out that students are assessed on how they prepare for and join class discussions.

_____Students try to solve tech problems before requesting help.

_____Show how to check grades online.

_____Discuss student responsibility to make up missed classes. Show where you post lesson plans.

_____Discuss passwords and privacy. Do not share logins with anyone. Have students save login info wherever it is secure. More on this in another lesson.

_____Discuss how to back up student work. Here are several options:

- *flash drives—students routinely save to the cloud and back-up to a flash drive they carry with them. If necessary, review how to use flash drives.*
- *a separate location—such as the hard drive on their laptop as well as the cloud (won't work with iPads or Chromebooks)*
- *email files to themselves—quick and easy back-up. Set up a file folder in the email account for 'backups'.*

_____For more on tech lessons, see articles at end of this lesson, *"10 Ways to be an Inquiry-based Teacher"*, *"11 Ways to Make an Inquiry-based Classroom"*, *"14 Factors to Consider for Tech Report Cards"*, *"7 Ways to Differentiate with Tech"*, and *"7 Ways to Assess Student Knowledge"*.

TOPIC ARTICLE

Class exit ticket: **Display on class screen a poll created (in PollDaddy, Google Forms or similar) and embedded into class website/wiki/blog. It lists 8th-grade tech topics. Students vote on which they think will be the most fun, most useful, or most exciting to learn. Leave poll open until next class.**

Differentiation

- *Add homework due dates to class online calendar for each month.*

NOTES:

_____

_____

_____

_____

_____

Computer Lab Manners and Responsibilities

Assignments / Homework

- Check class website each day.
- Read and respond to communications at least once a day.
- If an assignment is not completed in class, turn it in remotely from home by 6:00 pm the same day with no penalty.
- Late assignments are 10% off for each day late.

Behavior in the Lab

- Keep an open mind that *something new will be learned* each day.
- Have clean hands; keyboards are shared by everyone.
- No food or drinks allowed in lab
- When helping other students, use words. Do not take over their digital device.

Posting emails

- Always enter subject of email
- Start each email with a greeting. (e.g. Hi Mrs. *** or Dear Mr. ***)
- Use correct punctuation. Start each sentence with a capital, end with a period.
- Proofread email and check spelling every time.
- Show insight and intelligence when responding to a class discussion or commenting on a post.
- CC anyone mentioned in an email. That's polite
- Don't share private information in emails. They aren't secure!
- Don't be rude in emails. They aren't private.
- Don't use capitals—THIS IS SHOUTING

Article 1—Habits of Mind vs. CC vs. IB

Habits of Mind vs. Common core vs. IB

Pedagogic experts have spent an enormous amount of time attempting to unravel the definition of 'educated'. It used to be the 3 R's—reading, writing, and 'rithmetic. The problem with that metric is that, in the fullness of time, those who excelled in the three areas weren't necessarily the ones who succeeded. As long ago as the early 1900's, Teddy Roosevelt warned:

""C students rule the world."

It's the kids without their nose in a book that notice the world around them, make connections, and learn natively. They excel at activities that aren't the result of a GPA and an Ivy League college. Their motivation is often failure and taking the wrong path again and again. As Thomas Edison said:

""I have not failed. I've just found 10,000 ways that won't work."

Microsoft founder, Bill Gates, and Albert Einstein are poster children for that approach. Both became change agents in their fields despite following a non-traditional path.

In the face of mounting evidence, education experts accepted a prescriptive fact: student success is not measured by milestones like 'took a foreign language in fifth grade' or 'passed Algebra in high school' but by how s/he thinks. One curated list of cerebral skills that has become an education buzz word is Arthur L. Costa and Bena Kallick's list of sixteen what they call Habits of Mind (Copyright ©2000):

1. *Persisting*
2. *Managing impulsivity*
3. *Listening with Understanding and Empathy*
4. *Thinking Flexibly*
5. *Thinking about Thinking*
6. *Striving for Accuracy*
7. *Questioning and Posing Problems*
8. *Applying Past Knowledge to New Situations*
9. *Thinking and Communicating with Clarity and Precision*
10. *Gathering Data through All Senses*
11. *Creating, Imagining, Innovating*
12. *Responding with Wonderment and Awe*
13. *Taking Responsible Risks*
14. *Finding Humor*
15. *Thinking Interdependently*
16. *Remaining Open to Continuous Learning*

Together, these promote strategic reasoning, insightfulness, perseverance, creativity and craftsmanship.

But they're not new. They share the same goals with at least three other widely-used education systems: 1) Common Core (as close as America gets to national standards), 2) the International Baccalaureate (IB) program (a well-regarded international curriculum, much more popular outside the US than within), and 3) good ol' common sense. Below, I've listed each Habit of Mind with a brief explanation of what that means (in italics). I then point out connections to Common Core, the IB Program, and the common sense your grandma shared with you. The result is a compelling argument that education is less a data download and more a fitness program for our brains.

Persisting

Stick with a problem, even when it's difficult and seems hopeless.

Winston Churchill said, "Never, never, in nothing great or small, large or petty, never give in..." The same decade, Albert Einstein said:

> *"It's not that I'm so smart, it's just that I stay with problems longer."*

The Common Core is not a curriculum, rather a collection of forty-one overarching Standards in reading, writing, language, math, and speaking/listening that shape a student's quest for college and career. Sprinkled throughout are fundamental traits that go beyond the 3R's and delve deeply into the ability of a student to think. The math standards require students learn to 'persevere in solving problems'.

The IB Program has twelve attitudes that are fundamental to every learner: *appreciation, empathy, commitment, enthusiasm, confidence, independence, cooperation, integrity, creativity, respect, curiosity, and tolerance.* Students exhibiting the attitude of commitment persist in their own learning, persevere no matter the difficulties.

Managing Impulsivity

Consider options. Think before speaking.

Among his endless words of wisdom, Benjamin Franklin said:

> *"It is easier to suppress the first desire than to satisfy all that follow it."*

Common Core Standards tell us to 'Use appropriate tools strategically'.

Besides the twelve attitudes listed above, the IB Program names ten traits that profile a learner: *inquirer, knowledgeable, thinker, communicator, principled, open-minded, caring, a risk-taker, balanced, and reflective.* Students who are reflective give thoughtful consideration before acting.

For the rest of the article, visit Ask a Tech Teacher

Article 2—Class Warm-ups and Exit Tickets

Class Warm-ups and Exit Tickets

Warm-ups are given at the beginning of class to measure what students remember from prior lessons or know about a subject before jumping into a unit. They inform teachers how to optimize time by teaching what students need to learn, not wasting time on what students already know. They are a couple of minutes, can be delivered via a Discussion Board, blog comments, a Google Form, or many other methods.

Exit tickets are similar but assess what students learned **during** the lesson. In this way, teachers know if they should review material, find a different approach to teaching a topic, or students are ready to move on. Like Warm-ups, Exit tickets are a few minutes, and delivered in a wide variety of creative methods.

Here are a few examples:

Polls

Polls are quick ways to assess student understanding of the goal of your daily teaching. It measures student learning as much as lesson effectiveness. Polls are fast—three-five minutes—are anonymously graded and shared immediately with students. It lets everyone know if the big idea of the lesson is understood and if the essential questions have been answered.

These can be graded, but are usually used formatively, to determine organic class knowledge before moving on to other topics.

Tools: Socrative, PollDaddy, Google Forms
Time: a few minutes
Method: Formative assessment

Virtual Wall

Ask students a question and have them add their answer to a virtual wall.

Virtual walls are also great ideas for reviewing a subject prior to a summative assessment. Have each student post an important idea they got from the unit with significant required details.

Tools: Padlet, Linoit
Time: a few minutes
Method: Formative assessment

4 Things Every Teacher Must Teach and How

Teaching technology is not sharing a new subject, like Spanish or math. It's exploring an education tool, knowing how to use computers, IPads, the Internet, and other digital devices to serve learning goals. Sure, there are classes that teach MS Word and C++, but for most schools, technology is employed strategically and capably to achieve all colors of education.

Which gets me to the four subjects every teacher must teach, whether s/he's a math teacher, science, literacy, or technology. In today's education world, all of us teach—

- *vocabulary*
- *keyboarding*
- *digital citizenship*
- *research*

They used to be taught in isolation—*Fridays at 8:20, we learn vocabulary*—but not anymore. Now they must be blended into all subjects like ingredients in a cake, the result—college or career for the 21st century student. Four subjects that must be taught—and thanks to technology, CAN be with ease. Let me explain.

Vocabulary

Common Core requires that:

> **Students constantly build the transferable vocabulary they need to access grade level complex texts. This can be done effectively by spiraling like content in increasingly complex texts.**

Does that sound difficult? Think back to how you conquered vocabulary. As an adult, you rarely meet words you can't understand—unless you're chatting with William F. Buckley—and if you do, you decode it by analyzing prefixes, suffixes, roots, context. Failing that, e-dictionaries are available on all digital devices.

Teach your students to do the same: 1) decode the word using affixes, root, context; 2) research meaning

You might think that will grind the academic process to a halt, but truth, in age-appropriate texts, there are likely less than five unknown words per page. What you don't want to do is have students write down words for later investigation. That becomes a chore, cerebral excitement leeched like heat to a night desert sky. Much better to stop, decode, and move on.

As students work on a project in my classes, I see neighbors ask for help with a mysterious word (students are welcome to chat during class about academic topics), screens light up as students use the online dictionary to discover meaning, and words appear on the class screen as part of the backchannel Twitter stream. Seconds later, a definition will appear—someone's contribution. If it's wrong, invariably a student will correct it. Rarely, I jump in. Don't believe this works? Try it out.

Keyboarding

For years, I taught keyboarding as a separate activity. We warmed up class with 10-15 minutes of keyboarding augmented by 45 minutes a week of keyboard homework. I've revised my thinking. Since keyboarding benefits all classes, I make all teachers—including the librarian—my partners in this effort. I go into classrooms and show students the broad strokes of keyboarding posture, good habits, skills that will enable them to type fast and accurately enough to eventually—maybe third or fourth grade—use the keyboard without slowing down their thinking. That's a big deal and worth repeating—

Students must keyboard fast enough that they keep up with their thoughts.

That's about 25 words per minute. *Really?* Yes really. Sure, we think fast, but ruminating over a class question, essay, report is much [much] slower. 25-35 words per minute suffice.

I start students with mouse and keyboard familiarity in kindergarten and 1st grade, introduce the concept of hands and fingers in 2nd, and start speed and accuracy in 3rd. By 5th grade, they're good. This works because now, keyboarding is integrated across all classes, anytime students use a digital device with a keyboard. Now, all teachers pay as much attention to HOW students use the keyboard as WHAT is produced, focusing on:

- good posture, hands on home row (by 3rd grade)
- elbows at sides
- paced rhythm
- paper (if using one) to the side of keyboard
- eyes on screen (by 4th grade)
- no flying fingers or hands

Parents, too, are my partners. I communicate the same requirements to them with the hope they'll reinforce these at home. A reminder that assessments are often online gets their attention.

Digital Citizenship

It's frightening how much time students spend in an online world they consider safe, following links like blind streets to places most parent wouldn't take their child. Just as students have learned how to survive in a physical community of strangers, they must now learn to do the same in a digital neighborhood. Parents and teachers can't be everywhere and hiding children from danger doesn't teach them survival skills, so we must teach them how to live in this wild new online world.

For more, visit this article on Ask a Tech teacher

Article 4—7 Ways to Assess Student Knowledge

7 Ways to Assess Student Knowledge

This is always challenging, isn't it? Finding evidence that students have learned what you taught, that they can apply their knowledge to complex problems. How do you do this? Rubrics? Group projects? Posters? None sound worthy of the Common Core educational environ—and too often, students have figured out how to deliver within these guidelines while on auto-pilot.

Where can we find authentic assessments that are measurable yet student-centered, promote risk-taking by student and teacher alike, are inquiry-driven, and encourage students to take responsibility for his/her own learning? How do we assess a lesson plan in a manner that ensures students have learned what they need to apply to life, to new circumstances they will face when no teacher is at their elbow to nudge them the right direction?

Here are some of my favorite approaches:

Anecdotally

I observe their actions, their work, the way they are learning the skills I'm teaching. Are they engaged, making their best effort? Do they remember skills taught in prior weeks and apply them? Do they self-assess and make corrections as needed?

Transfer of knowledge

Can students transfer knowledge learned in my class to other classes and/or other parts of their life? Do I hear fun stories from parents and teachers about how students used something learned? Do the students themselves share a snippet about how they 'helped mom use Google Maps to find...'?

Teach others

Are students comfortable flipping learning and becoming the teacher? There's a hierarchy of learning that goes like this:

1. *Student doesn't listen*
2. *Student doesn't believe*
3. *Student tries it once*
4. *Student remembers it*
5. *Student shows it to others*
6. *Student teaches others*

Like Maslow's Hierarchy of Needs, the highest praise is that students teach the skill to others. That's learning.

I encourage it in my classes by having the lab open during recess and lunch, but with students as helpers. I only take 1-2 and always have more offers than I need.

Verbalize

Can students use the right words to share answers? No umms, no hand motions, no giggles. Can they take a deep breath and share their knowledge in a few succinct sentences? This works well on a Discussion Board which I use as a summative for vocabulary and problem-solving tests. I set up a discussion board, ask each student to add a problem or vocabulary word we covered, and then comment on a classmate's. They can then use this resource during the test. We've done it a few times and students have figured out if they blow off the Discussion Board part of the assessment, everyone suffers. Friends don't have the study guide, or worse, the answer's wrong because classmates didn't take the time to write it correctly.

Portfolio

I like portfolios, but today, that means digital. Collect all student work onto wikis, digital lockers, Box.net, via embed widgets or screenshots or the original software. Keep it in the cloud where students, teachers, even parents can access it. That's transparency. No one will wonder what grade the student earned

Summarize knowledge

But not in an essay. Use knowledge to create a magazine, an Animoto video, a PuzzleMaker crossword. It's the 'use' part of assessment that's most important. Can students use the knowledge or does it just sit in a mental file folder?

Oral presentations

This can be summative, formative, informational, or informal. It can be a quick answer to questions in the classroom, coming up to the class screen and solving a problem, teaching classmates how to solve a problem during class, or preparing a multimedia presentation to share with others online or in person. It includes much more than an assessment of learning. It judges a student's presentation skills, ability to talk to people—life skills fundamental.

In the end, the choice of assessment depends upon the goal of teaching. Which works best for you?

10 Ways to be an Inquiry-based Teacher

It's hard to run an inquiry-based classroom. Don't go into this teaching style thinking all you do is ask questions and observe answers. You have to listen with all of your senses, pause and respond to what you heard (not what you wanted to hear), keep your eye on the Big Ideas as you facilitate learning, value everyone's contribution, be aware of the energy of the class and step in when needed, step aside when required. You aren't a Teacher, rather a guide. You and the class move from question to knowledge together.

Because everyone learns differently.

Where your teacher credential classes taught you to use a textbook, now it's one of many resources. Sure, it nicely organizes knowledge week-by-week, but in an inquiry-based classroom, you may know where you're going, but not quite how you'll get there—and that's a good thing. You are no longer your mother's teacher who stood in front of rows of students and pointed to the blackboard. You operate well outside your teaching comfort zone as you try out a flipped classroom and the gamification of education and are thrilled with the results.

And then there's the issue of assessment. What students accomplish can no longer neatly be summed up by a multiple choice test. When you review what you thought would assess learning (back when you designed the unit), none measure the organic conversations the class had about deep subjects, the risk-taking they engaged in to arrive at answers, the authentic knowledge transfer that popped up independently of your class time. You realize you must open your mind to learning that occurred that you never taught—never saw coming in the weeks you stood amongst your students guiding their education.

Let me digress. I visited the Soviet Union (back when it was one nation) and dropped in on a classroom where students were inculcated with how things must be done. It was a polite, respectful, ordered experience, but without cerebral energy, replete of enthusiasm for the joy of learning, and lacking the wow factor of students independently figuring out how to do something. Seeing the end of that powerful nation, I arrived at different conclusions than the politicians and the economists. I saw a nation starved to death for creativity. Without that ethereal trait, learning didn't transfer. Without transfer, life required increasingly more scaffolding and prompting until it collapsed in on itself like a hollowed out orange.

So how do you create the inquiry-based classroom? Here's advice from a few of my efriend teachers:

1. *Ask open-ended questions and be open-minded about conclusions.*
2. *Provide hands-on experiences.*
3. *Use groups to foster learning.*
4. *Encourage self-paced learning. Be open to the student who learns less but deeper as much as the student who learns a wider breadth.*
5. *Differentiate instruction. Everyone learns in their own way.*
6. *Look for evidence of learning in unusual places. It may be from the child with his/her hand up, but it may also be from the learner who teaches mom how to use email.*

7. *Understand 'assessment' comes in many shapes. It may be a summative quiz, a formative simulation, a rubric, or a game that requires knowledge to succeed. It may be anecdotal or peer-to-peer. Whatever approach shows students are transferring knowledge from your classroom to life is a legitimate assessment.*
8. *Be flexible. Class won't always (probably never) go as your mind's eye saw it. That's OK. Learn with students. Observe their progress and adapt to their path.*
9. *Give up the idea that teaching requires control. Refer to #8—Be flexible.*
10. *Facilitate student learning in a way that works for them. Trust that they will come up with the questions required to reach the Big Ideas.*

In the end, know that inquiry-based teaching is not about learning for the moment. You're creating life-long learners, the individuals who will solve the world's problems in ten years. Your job is to ensure they are ready.

11 Ways to Make an Inquiry-based Classroom

You became a teacher not to pontificate to trusting minds, but to teach children how to succeed as adults. That idealism infused every class in your credential program and only took a slight bump during your student teacher days. That educator, you figured, was a dinosaur. You'd never teach to the test or lecture for forty minutes of a forty-five minute class.

Then you got a job and reality struck. You had lesson plans to get through, standards to assess, and state-wide tests that students must do well on or you'd get the blame. A glance in the mirror said you were becoming that teacher you hated in school. You considered leaving the profession.

Until the inquiry-based classroom arrived where teaching's goal was not the solution to a problem, but the path followed. It's what you'd hoped to do long ago when you started—but how do you turn a traditional entrenched classroom into one that's inquiry-based?

One step at a time, and here are fifteen you can take. One or more will resonate with your teaching style:

Flip the classroom

The night prior to the lesson, have students read the lecture materials so you can spend class time in hands-on discovery.

Don't answer student questions—show them how to do it themselves.

When students have questions, you guide them toward answers. Don't give them a fish, rather teach them to fish. When students understand the methodology, they can repeat the process. Without understanding, they are robots.

But this requires comprehensive teacher preparation to be ready for the multitude of directions a conversation can go, not just steer student inquiry where you're comfortable. Inquiry-based lessons are process-, not product-oriented. How students reach conclusions is as important as the conclusions they reach. That critical thinking is what it's about. Think back to your favorite school lessons. Were they learning the capital of every state or where you came to understand the scientific method? (OK, maybe that comparison doesn't work, but you get my point—likely, your favorite lessons required you to think, not regurgitate).

Listen when students speak

It's tempting to think you know what students are going to ask/say. Resist the impulse. Listen. Try to understand what their real question is, not what their words say. Watch them. Are they comfortable with your answer, or does it make them squirm? Take the time to travel the distance to a solution.

Encourage questions.

Class is ticking away and there are too many questions. If you take time to answer all of them, you won't cover the material scheduled.

That's OK. Take the time. Make the issues clear. An odd thing will start to happen. As students more thoroughly understand a concept, they will transfer that knowledge to other lessons and those will go faster than expected. By the end of the year, you'll have covered more material in more depth. Cool, hunh?

Spend time on projects, not lecturing

There's an old Chinese proverb, although Ben Franklin occasionally gets credit for these words:

"Tell me and I'll forget.
Show me and I may remember.
Involve me and I'll understand."

Inquiry is about doing, not observing, action not inaction.

Lessons are fluid

Learning isn't linear. It's a web that grows out from the central question. As such, your lesson plan may change dramatically based on student inquiry. If you teach three fifth grade classes, each will likely be different from the other. That's OK. Your challenge is to track what you did in each class and pick up from where you left off. That's OK, too. It's part of the job of teaching an inquiry-based class.

For more on this article, visit Ask a Tech Teacher

14 Factors to Consider for Tech Report Cards

It used to be simple to post grades. Add up test scores and see what the student earned. Very defensible. Everyone understood.

It's not that way anymore. Here are the factors I consider when I'm posting grades:

- Does s/he remember skills from prior lessons as they complete current lessons?
- Does s/he show evidence of learning by using tech class knowledge in classroom or home?
- Does s/he participate in class discussions?
- Does s/he complete daily goals (a project, visit a website, watch a tutorial, etc.)?
- Does s/he save to their digital portfolio?
- Does s/he try to solve tech problems themselves before asking for teacher help?
- Does s/he use core classroom knowledge (i.e., writing conventions) in tech projects?
- Does s/he work well in groups?
- Does s/he use the internet safely?
- Does s/he [whichever Common Core Standard is being pursued by the use of technology. It may be 'able to identify shapes' in first grade or 'able to use technology to add audio' in fourth grade]?
- Does s/he display creativity and critical thinking in the achievement of goals?
- Has student progressed at keyboarding skills?
- Anecdotal observation of student learning (this is subjective and enables me to grade students based on effort)
- Grades on tests, quizzes, projects

I'm tempted to put everything in a spreadsheet, award a value, calculate a total and find an average. Then—Magic! I have a grade! It's risk-averse, explainable to parents and Admin, a comfort zone of checklists and right-and-wrong answers. But I know I can't do that. In an inquiry-based classroom, too much is a subjective analysis, a personal evaluation of the student's uniqueness. I can't—and don't want to—get away from that approach.

What do you use that I haven't mentioned? I'm already thinking ahead to the next grading period.

Article 8—7 Ways to Differentiate with Tech

7 Ways to Differentiate with Tech

There are two areas where technology can optimize learning better than any other educational strategy. I'm not talking about iPads or laptops or apps. I mean how you deliver your message—done in such a way that more students are able to achieve their goals.

The first is **problem solving**. If you want students to be critical thinkers, to take responsibility for their own learning and in doing so, excel—and you do—you must must MUST use technology to teach problem solving. More on that later.

Today, we'll talk about **differentiation**. If you struggle to adapt your lessons to the multitude of learning styles in your classroom, struggle no more. Technology is like that friendly laugh that diffuses a tense situation, the tale wag from a Rottweiler to tell you s/he's on your side. Tech will become your classroom's transformative tool—a magic wand that can adapt any inquiry to student needs. Take the cornerstone of literacy—the book report—as an example. When a teacher assigns this sort of compare/contract, who/what/when/where exercise, students thinks paragraphs of words and grammar struggles. Thanks to technology, that project is no longer a nightmare for everyone challenged by phrases and paragraphs. Now, students have options that transcend pencil on paper. Communicate the essential ideas with a comic tool like Storyboard That!, an art tool like SumoPaint. How about an audio tool like Voki—or a movie maker like Animoto. The challenge for you as teacher is to provide those tech options and then encourage students to be risk-takers in using them to achieve the project goals. The challenge for students is to analyze what's available and select the tool that uses their learning style.

You're probably thinking that before students can use these fancy tools, you have to learn all of them—and teach them. Where's that sort of time come from—and by the way, you aren't one of the 'techie' teachers. Do I have good news for you. The ideas below require very little prep from you. Students learn to read the screen, look for something that says 'start', not be afraid to make mistakes, and collaborate with neighbors on the learning. This can happen as young as 2nd grade. The hardest part for you is to facilitate rather than step in and solve their problems. Students will get used to the new reality that teachers provide guidance not step-by-step instruction. I promise.

Here are seven ways to differentiate instruction every day:

1. Does this scenario sound familiar: While some students carefully finish a project, taking their time as suits their learning style, others slam through the steps and start looking for 'what's next'. You know the type. Both approaches are fine. Address it by having a lot of authentic activities going on in your classroom so students are encouraged to work at their own pace. Let them self-manage their education. Be clear about your expectations, and then trust them to find their way. Have links on the class internet start page for organic learning like keyboarding practice and sponge websites that tie into subject area inquiry.

2. Teach students how to create visual organizers, and then let them use these optionally for projects. These can be graphic organizers like Venn Diagrams or pyramids, or an infographic made in Easel.ly. Let them communicate their ideas with not only text, but layout, color, and images. That appeals to the artist in lots of students.

3. Add color to everything. If you're using Word (or Google Docs), show students how to add pictures, borders, fonts. Students will tolerate the words to get to the decorating. If you're teaching Excel, show how to color cells, text, add images. They'll do the math stuff so they can make it pretty.

4. Use online tools like Discovery Education's Puzzle Maker to review concepts. Move away from rubrics and study guides. Anything that gamifies learning will go down easier with students. They are digital natives so let them learn in a more natural way.

5. In fact, gamify anything possible. There are an amazing number of high-quality simulations that teach through play—Minecraft, iCivics, Mission US, Lemonade Stand. Here's a long list. There's probably one for every subject. Take advantage of them.

6. If students aren't excited by the tools and widgets you offer, let them suggest their own. If they can make the argument for it, let them use it.

7. Always offer do-overs. I call them 'Mulligans' (from golf). In a differentiated classroom, you always want to let students redo an assignment. What if they didn't understand? Or were sick? How does trying harder defeat education's goal of learning? With technology, all students have to do is open their project and continue work based on your feedback. That's cool. Rest assured: When you offer this in your classroom, most students won't take you up on it. It's too outside-the-box. You won't be deluged with double the work. But be happy if you are.

That's it. Try these seven ideas and see if they don't transform your classroom. Questions? Email me (or leave a comment).

Lesson #2 Digital Tools in the Classroom

Vocabulary	Problem solving	Homework
• Annotation • App • Backchannel • Benchmark • Blog • Cloud • Digital portfolio • Digital tools • Domain-specific • Hashtag • Linkback • PDF • Plagiarism • Template	• I'm too young for Twitter (use class account) • Avatar didn't show in my blog (ask a neighbor how they did it) • My work disappeared (Google Apps automatically saves; or Ctrl+Z) • Teacher isn't around and I need help (ask for peer support or student forum) • Just give me a handout (Sorry, we learn through experience and collaboration) • I'm not fast enough decoding vocabulary (keep at it—it gets easier) • I forgot my Evidence (you'll have a chance every month)	Preview/test tech tools and compare-contrast tables; prepare presentation Log in from home/school Prepare for hardware quiz and Summative Keyboard 45 min., 15 minutes a time Find and take poll.
Academic Applications Writing, research, collaboration, publishing	**Required skills** blogs, annotate PDFs, hardware, avatars, portfolios, email, vocab decoding tools, keyboarding	**Standards** CCSS: WHST.6-8.7-9 NETS: 1b, 4b

Essential Question

How do I use technology to pursue my education?

Big Idea

Students become aware of how tech enhances educational goals

Teacher Preparation/Materials Required

- Have back channel available.
- Have copies (if required) of hardware assessment.
- Talk with grade-level team to tie into conversations.
- Have student accounts for digital tools.
- Have Evidence Board and badges prepared.
- Post links to training videos on digital tools (if using).
- Have copies of blogging agreement (if necessary).
- Integrate domain-specific tech vocabulary into the lesson.
- Something happen you didn't expect? Show how you fix the emergency with a positive attitude.

Assessment Strategies

- Previewed required material; came to class prepared
- Annotated workbook (if using)
- Used good keyboarding habits
- Completed warm-up, exit ticket
- Completed lesson summative
- Joined classroom conversations
- [tried to] solve own problems
- Decisions followed class rules
- Left room as s/he found it
- Higher order thinking: analysis, evaluation, synthesis
- Habits of mind observed

Steps

Time required: *90 minutes or more, spread throughout the school year*
Class warm-up: *Keyboarding on the class typing program*

_____Homework is assigned the week before this unit so students are prepared.

_____Any questions from homework? Expect students to review unit and come to class prepared.

_____Ask what tech problems students had difficulty with.

_____Discuss results of interest poll (Exit Ticket from *Lesson #1*).

_____Discuss digital tools in general terms. What are they? How are they different from software? Consider these differences (*Figure 9*):

Figure 9—Compare-contrast software vs. online tool

	SOFTWARE	ONLINE TOOL
Examples	MS Office, KidPix, Type to Learn, Reader Rabbit	Google Drive apps, ABCYa, Dance Mat Typing
Access	Accessible only from where you installed the software	Accessible from any computer with an internet connection
Compatibility	Varies	Most are compatible across platforms (Windows, Macs, Linux, Chromebooks)
Control	You control	Someone else controls—may be moved or removed without your permission
Cost	Varies	Varies—often free versions are available
Daily use	Depends upon whether your computer works and whether the software is compatible with changes you've made to your computer	Depends upon whether your internet connection works
Limitation	Don't run on iPads, Chromebooks	Run on most computer systems
Maintenance	If it breaks, you have to fix it	If it breaks, someone online fixes it
Security	As secure as your computer is	Depends upon the website's security
Set-up	You must install; might require adaptations to work on your system	No installation required—all you do is go to the site
Speed	Depends upon your system	Depends upon your internet connection
Updates	You do these	Managed by website; always up to date
Where it lives	On your computer (or network)	On the internet
Working with a partner	Difficult	Easy

_____How about apps? How are they different from software and online tools? Which have students used? Why have they become mainstays in life? See if students come up with ideas such as:

- *to facilitate collaborative work*
- *to enable students easily publish and share a project with classmates*
- *to make communication with multiple audiences easier*
- *to enable use of a wide variety of media and formats*
- *to encourage cultural understanding and global awareness*
- *to provide options (for example: for communication—email, forums, blogs)*
- *to provide access from anywhere with an internet connection*

_____This *Digital Tools* unit has three expected learning outcomes:

- *introduce digital tools to be used in 8ᵗʰ grade*
- *acclimate students to the concept that tech tools enable differentiation, collaboration, sharing, and publishing*
- *show how to employ them in student educational endeavors*

_____Before reviewing digital tools to be used during class, have neighbors check each other's mouse hold (see *Figure 10*):

Figure 10—How to hold a mouse

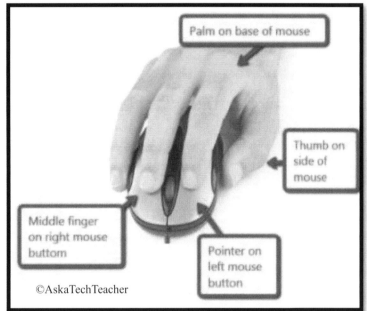

_____Review your school digital device. Students should know the basic parts and whether they're input or output. *Figures 11a-d* are images of assessments at the end of this Lesson. These can be filled out in student workbooks during classtime. *Figures 12a-b* are sample completed worksheets.

Figure 11a-d—Digital devices and their parts

  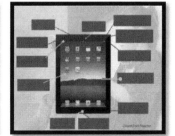 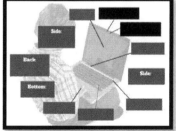

_____If necessary, review with students. For example, if you use iPads, ask where the headphones are on this device? Or the mouse? How about the USB Port? Ask students where the iPad microphone is on, say, the PC or Chromebook. How about the charging dock?

Figure 12a—Parts of iPad; 12b—Chromebook

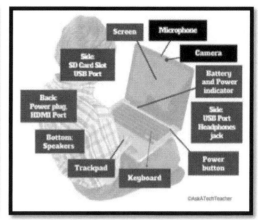

_____Discuss how understanding hardware helps to solve tech problems. Ask students if they have any personal examples—how they were able to debug hardware issues at home to fix a problem.

_____Discuss digital citizenship in broad strokes. Remind students of rights and responsibilities inherent to the digital community. You focus on it in another lesson and return to it every time students use internet.

_____These tools are discussed in this lesson. Pick those your students use; add others you have:

- *annotation tool*
- *avatars*
- *backchannel devices*
- *blogs*
- *class calendar*
- *class Internet start page*
- *class Twitter account*
- *class website*
- *digital note-taking*
- *digital portfolios*
- *dropbox*

- *email*
- *Evidence Board*
- *flipped classroom*
- *Google Apps and maps*
- *online quizzes*
- *screenshots and screencasts*
- *student websites*
- *student workbooks*
- *study helper*
- *video channel*
- *vocabulary decoding tools*

_____Select one student or a group to review each tool with class (with material prepared for homework). Discuss what must be known to use the tool (i.e., log in, location). Include information in articles on blogging and twitter. Ask clarifying questions. Fill in blanks where needed. Be sure information from the rest of this Unit is included.

_____Adapt the tools and activities to your digital devices (Chromebooks, PCs, iMac, iPads, or other).

_____At the lesson end, there's a summative project.

Student workbooks

_____If using the student workbooks that go along with this curriculum, show how to:

- *open on digital device*
- *find rubrics and project samples; take quizzes; complete rubrics*
- *take notes using the annotation tool*

Annotation Tool and Screenshots

_____If using student workbooks, show students how to annotate their copy with the note-taking tool used in your school such as those in Figure 13a-c:

Figure 13a—iAnnotate; 13b—Notability; 13c—Adobe Acrobat

 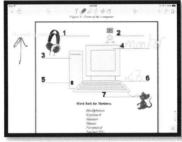 

_____If students share the PDF (for example, it's loaded on a digital device that multiple students use), show how to select their own color that's different from other students.

_____Include a discussion of screenshots. Often, students will annotate a page (say, a rubric) and then save a screenshot of it to their digital portfolio. Depending upon your digital device, you'll use a screenshot tool like one of these:

- ***Windows****: the Snipping Tool*
- ***Chromebook:*** *hold down the control key and press the window switcher key*
- ***Mac****: Command Shift 3 to do a full screenshot and Command Shift 4 for a partial*
- ***Surface tablet****: hold down volume and Windows button at the same time*
- ***iPad****: hold Home button and power button at same time*
- ***Online****: a screenshot tool like Jing or Snagit*

_____Point out to students that the annotation tool not only allows them to note-take in the curriculum book, but any PDF they access with their digital device.

_____Show how students can use a web-based annotation tool (like Snagit or Nimbus—Google for addresses) to mark up a web page and then save a copy to student digital portfolio.

Avatars

_____Students can create a profile picture with an avatar creator from Voki, Storyboard That, or another (Google for address—*Figures 14a-d* are examples).

Figure 14a-d—Avatars

_____Discuss the fact that avatars should look nothing like students and include nothing that can be tied back to the student. Consider this the student's alter-ego. For example, if the student has blue eyes, their avatar should have brown.

_____These can be used in student wikis, websites, or any digital platform that requires a profile picture. Use them to reinforce a discussion of digital privacy and safety.

Backchannel Devices

_____The 'backchannel' is classroom communication that isn't from the presenter. 'Backchannel devices' encourage students to share their thoughts and ideas, even questions, while a lesson is going on. Typically, the comments show up on the class screen, shared with all classmates, likely anonymously. Students read and respond. You use them to be informed when students get/don't get a topic s/he is covering.

_____Popular backchannel options are (do an Internet search for website):

- *Padlet_—Figure 15a*
- *Socrative—Figure 15b*
- *Twitter*

Figure 15a-b—Backchannel devices

_____Why use backchannels? Here are a few reasons:

- *you know what engages students and extend those ideas*
- *you hear from shy students who need a classroom voice*
- *gregarious students can ask as much as they want without dominating class*

_____Introduce the backchannel to students and demo, and then use it as you introduce the balance of the digital tools. Student feedback will inform whether you teach or review the digital tools.

Blogs

_____Blogs are short online articles with the purpose of sharing ideas and garnering feedback. In 8th grade, you are particularly interested in the facility to:

- *engage effectively in collaborative discussions with diverse partners*
- *build on others' ideas*
- *express their own ideas clearly*

_____Review the articles at lesson end on *13 Ways Blogs Teach Common Core* and *8 Things my Blog Taught Me.*

_____*Figures 16a-c* are examples of student blogs. Notice how posts incorporate text and images:

Figure 16a-c—Student blogs

_____Student blogs teach writing skills, how to use evidence to support arguments (in both posts and comments), and perspective-taking. They are student-directed, but you approve both posts and comments until students get used to the rules that apply to online conversations.

_____Blogs reflect student personalities with colors, fonts, and widgets. What students include will help you better understand how they learn and how to reach them academically.

_____In general, student blogs require:

- *titles that pull reader in and a tone/voice that fits this type of writing*
- *linkback(s) to evidence that supports statements*
- *at least one media to support each article (picture, video, sound)*
- *understanding of target audience, purpose. How is it different from tweets? Essays? Poetry?*
- *citations—authors name, permission, linkbacks, and copyright where required*
- *occasional teamwork*
- *pithy content with correct spelling and grammar and no slang*

_____Before beginning, students sign an agreement similar to *Figure 17a*—full size at end of lesson. Ask them to discuss the agreement with parents and bring it to school before the next class. If you're using workbooks, students can sign the copy in there, take a screenshot, and email that to you.

Figure 17a—Blogging rules; 17b—blogging rubric

_____Students can create blogs in WordPress, Class Blogmeister, Blogger (Google for addresses; Blogger comes with Google Apps). They can be public or private.

_____Discuss blogging netiquette—similar to email etiquette:

- *be polite*
- *use good grammar and spelling*
- *don't write anything everyone shouldn't read (school blogs are private, but get students used to the oxymoron of privacy and the Internet)*

_____Have students test their blog log-in and add their first 'Hello!' post. Remind them to practice good keyboarding as they type.

_____Once a month, have students post an article that discusses an inquiry topic. Additionally, students should visit and comment on five classmate blogs.

_____Student comments aren't always appropriate? Set account so you approve comments before they're live. And chat about how supportive comments contribute to the conversation.

_____Occasionally throughout the year, use the Student Blog Rubric *(Figure 17b*—full-size assessment at end of the lesson) to assess student progress.

Class Calendar

_____Class calendars can be through Google Apps or another tool that works for your student group. Show students how to access it and how it's updated to reflect class activities.

_____If students will edit, demonstrate how to do this by adding upcoming homework.

_____Encourage students to contribute responsibly to class calendar.

_____If using Google Apps, students can embed calendar into blogs, websites, or wikis.

_____For Google Calendar training, visit Google's comprehensive calendar training.

Class Internet Start Page

_____An Internet start page is a website that comes up when the student opens the Internet. It organizes critical content in a single location and curates links students will use.

_____Include what students visit daily (i.e., guidelines, calendar, 'to do' list, typing websites, research locations, sponge sites, calculator) as well as information specific to the current project.

_____You might also include pictures of interest, RSS feeds, weather, a graffiti wall, and a class pet.

Figure 18—Class Internet start page

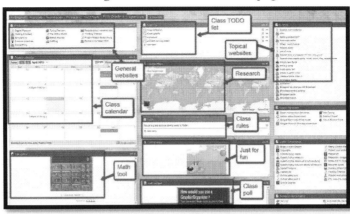

_____Use Protopage.com_*(Figure 18)*, Ighome, or a collection site like Symbaloo_*(Figure 19a)*, Portaportal_*(Figure 19b)*, LiveBinders *(Figure 19c)*, Diigo, or the class Evernote account (Google names for address).

Figure 19a—Class start page in Symbaloo; 19b—Portaportal; 19c—LiveBinders

_____Remind students that any time they visit the Internet, do so safely and legally. This will be discussed in depth in another lesson.

_____See article at end of this lesson, ***Class Internet Start Page***.

Class Twitter account

_____Discuss article at end of this lesson, ***"13 Ways Twitter Improves Education"***.

_____Twitter is a natural in the 8th grade classroom. It is hip. Students want to check their stream to see what's up. Because tweets must be concise, they are an excellent way to teach writing.

_____Like blogs and wikis, Twitter feeds are used to:

- *engage collaboratively with diverse partners*
- *review key ideas*
- *present findings with descriptions, facts, and details*
- *pose questions that elicit elaboration*
- *acknowledge information from others*

_____Set up a private class twitter account for announcements, _____group questions, discussions, notetaking, quiz preparation, and collaboration. Use #hashtags to organize themes like #homework, #class, #questions, and whatever works for your student group.

_____Most blog and website activity can also be tweeted, so it's a great redundancy for getting news where it needs to go.

_____If you prefer, rather than a class Twitter account, have students create their own and join class Twitter feed. Before leaving this section, have each student tweet hello to classmates using #hashtag *#introductions*.

Class Website

_____Class websites serve as a general resource collection for class information. This is maintained by the teacher, but you may (or not) include students in managing, updating, and posting to the class site.

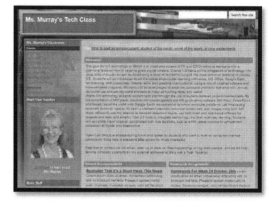

_____Class websites include much of the same information that the Internet start page does, but in more detail. For example, you can include information on upcoming field trips with sign-up forms and parent permission slips. You can include links to class events.

_____Some of the popular items you can include pm a class websites are:

- *polls*
- *discussion boards*
- *forums*
- *teacher picture and bio*
- *links to class activities*
- *class expectations, standards*
- *link to grades*

_____Create this using the same tool that students will use for their student blog or website.

Digital Note-taking

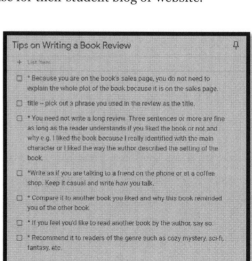

_____What are some of the reasons to take notes (from Common Core):

- *determine central ideas*
- *provide accurate summary*
- *identify key steps*
- *cite text evidence to support analysis*
- *analyze structure used to organize text*
- *analyze author's purpose*

_____Here are five digital note-taking methods:

Figure 20a-b—Note-taking tools—word processing and Notability

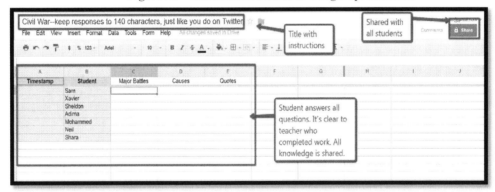

- *Word processing program (for any digital device) – Figure 20a*
- *Notability (for iPads) – Figure 20b*
- *Google Apps – (for any digital device) — Figure 21 (zoom in for detail)*

Figure 21—Collaborative notes in Google Spreadsheets

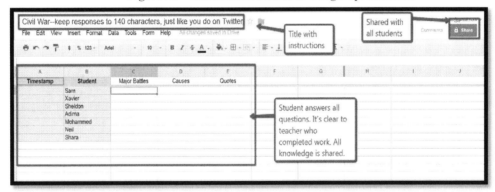

- *Evernote/OneNote (for most digital devices) — Figure 22a*
- *Twitter (for most digital devices) — Figure 22b*

Figure 22a—Evernote; 22b—Twitter

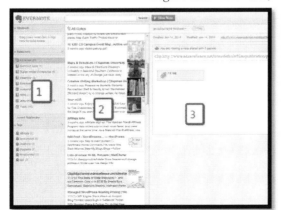
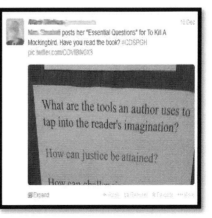

Digital portfolios

_____Discuss how students use digital portfolios (also known as digital lockers or digital binders):

- *store work (in Cloud) required in other classes or at home*
- *interact, collaborate, and publish with peers, experts, or others*
- *edit or review work in multiple locations*
- *submit class assignments*

_____There are a variety of approaches to digital portfolios that satisfy some or all of the above uses: 1) folders on school network, 2) fee-based programs from companies such as Richer Picture, 3) cloud-based storage like Dropbox or Google Apps *(Figure 23b),* and 4) online collaborative sites like PBWorks.com (Google for addresses).

_____Review *Assessment* rubric at lesson's end on what should be included in a digital portfolio.

_____Occasionally, use the *Assessment* to review student progress with their own digital portfolio.

Figure 23a—Wiki; 23b—Google Drive

Dropbox

_____A classwork and homework drop box can be created through the school Learning Management System (LMS), email, Google Apps (through the 'share' function), Google Classroom, or other options. In fact, any alternative to submitting print homework is good.

_____If you use this, review it. If not, show how students submit classwork and homework.

Figure 24—Homework dropbox

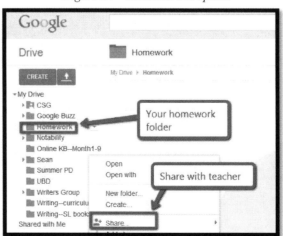

_____If necessary, create a Homework drop box like *Figure 24*:

- *Each student creates a folder called 'Homework' that is shared with you.*
- *To submit work to you, copy it to that folder so you can view and comment.*

Email

_____Use a web-based account such as Gmail (comes with GAFE and Google Classrooms).

_____Review email etiquette (*Figure 25*—full-size poster in Appendix):

- *Use proper writing conventions.*
- *CC anyone mentioned.*
- *Make 'Subject line' topic of email.*
- *Answer swiftly.*
- *Re-read before sending.*
- *Don't use all caps—THIS IS SHOUTING.*
- *Don't attach unnecessary files.*
- *Don't overuse high priority.*
- *Don't email confidential information.*
- *Don't email offensive remarks.*
- *Don't forward chain letters or spam.*
- *Don't open attachments from strangers.*

Figure 25—Email etiquette

EMAIL ETIQUETTE

1. Use proper formatting, spelling, grammar
2. CC anyone you mention
3. Subject line is what your email discusses
4. Answer swiftly
5. Re-read email before sending
6. Don't use capitals—THIS IS SHOUTING
7. Don't leave out the subject line
8. Don't attach unnecessary files
9. Don't overuse high priority
10. Don't email confidential information
11. Don't email offensive remarks
12. Don't forward chain letters or spam
13. Don't open attachments from strangers

_____If you have student email accounts, review how to use them.

_____Clarify terms like 'high priority', 'chain letters', and 'CC'.

_____Let students (and parents) know that the email program they use at home may not match the instructions you've provided. Ask parents to show students how to use the home-based email.

_____Why is correct grammar/spelling important in email and not so much with texting? Hint: Consider this Common Core standard: *Produce clear and coherent writing in which development, organization, and style are appropriate to task and audience.*

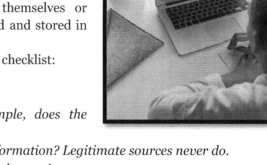

_____Discuss 'spam'. What is it? Why is it sent? What should students do when spam shows up in their email? Show how to manage settings so students don't get spam.

_____Discuss how email can be used to back-up important documents (by emailing a copy to themselves or creating a draft email with doc attached and stored in 'Draft' file).

_____When students get an email, follow this checklist:

- *Do you know sender?*
- *Is email legitimate? For example, does the 'voice' sound like sender?*
- *Is sender asking for personal information? Legitimate sources never do.*
- *Is there an attachment? If so, don't open it.*

Evidence Board

_____The Evidence Board (*Figure 26a*) is a bulletin board that celebrates student transfer of knowledge from tech class to home, friends, or other educational endeavors.

_____About once a month, students share how they use tech skills outside of your class. They make a ten-second presentation to class, fill out a badge (like *Figure 26b*), and post it on the Evidence Board by their class. By year end, you want this collection to encircle the classroom.

Figure 26a—Evidence Board; 26b—Badge

Flipped Classroom

_____What is a flipped classroom (see *Figures 27a-b*—zoom in if needed)? In the Flipped Classroom (as used in this curriculum), teachers record their lectures for consumption by students outside of class, and then dedicate class time to project-based learning that supports the homework. This approach allows students to ask questions of their teacher or collaborate with peers *as they're doing the work*, rather than struggling with it at home and asking for help the next day.

Figure 27a—Blendspace; 27b—flipped class definition

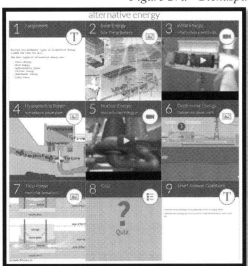 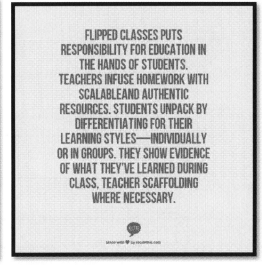

_____Show students where they'll find their homework (probably on the class website or blog or pushed out through Google Classroom) and model how they will complete it.
_____Likely, it will include several pieces:

- *summary video prepared by you*
- *reading material from ebooks or online sources*
- *hands-on work such as keyboard practice*
- *preparatory steps required to participate in the classtime project*

_____Tools you might use for the summary video include (do an Internet search for website):

- YouTube channel
- Periscope
- Vialogues
- Touchcast

_____Tools you might use to collect homework materials for students are:

- Blendspace
- Google Classroom
- Lesson Paths

Google Apps

_____To access Google Apps requires an account. *Figure 28* is what Google Drive might look like:

Figure 28—Google Apps

_____There are many resources available for teaching how to use Google Apps. If you have trouble finding one, check the list on Ask a Tech Teacher's resource pages.

_____Give students time to explore Google Drive before moving on.

_____The most popular apps—and the ones students will use the most—are:

- *Google Docs—for word processing projects*
- *Google Slides—for slideshow presentations*
- *Google Spreadsheets—for the analysis of data using spreadsheets*
- *Google Draw—for visual representation of information*

Maps

_____Create maps of events, literature, history, and more. Have a map making app or site available for any time students need to map out class inquiry locations or track events in a novel:

Figure 29—A mapmaker

Online Quizzes

_____Use an online quiz tool from the resource pages on Ask a Tech Teacher.

_____You can also use Google Forms (part of Google Apps for Education). It doesn't matter which as long as students get used to taking quizzes and being graded online and getting immediate feedback (often). This will be a growing part of Common Core assessment so you want students used to it.

Screenshots and Screencasts

_____Review detail under '*Annotation and Screenshots*'.

_____Students will use screenshot (still images—*Figure 30a*) tools, apps, or add-ons (depending upon your digital device), as well as screencasts (videos—*Figure 30b*) to record information from their screen. More on this in the lesson on '*Screenshots and Screencasts*'.

Figure 30a—Screenshot to explain log-in; 30b—screencast to explain the use of screencasts

 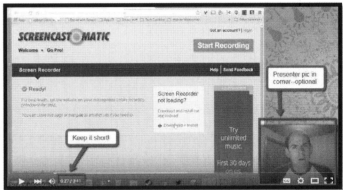

Student website

_____Most teachers will select either blogs or websites for students, depending upon their goal:

- *Blogs are more interactive and time-sensitive.*
- *Websites more fully cover a topic and new posts don't push older out of the way.*

_____Like blogs, websites are a great way to encourage reflection, organization, logical thinking, and are a perfect place to embed sharable projects, i.e., Tagxedos and Animotos.

_____Websites are available with Google Apps. If your school doesn't have Google Apps, free websites can be created at Weebly, Wix, or blog accounts like WordPress (Google for addresses).

_____Websites reflect student personalities with colors, fonts, and layout. Encourage creativity.

_____In general:

- *Website and article titles pull readers in.*
- *Articles review what readers can expect, provide evidence with supporting links, and include a summary of content.*
- *Tone/voice fits this type of writing and intended audience.*
- *Links connect to evidence and links work.*

- *At least one media is provided to support each article (picture, video, sound).*
- *Posts understand target audience. How are website readers different from Tweeting? Or writing essays?*
- *Writing purpose is clear. How is that different from tweets? Essays? Poetry?*
- *Citations are included as needed.*
- *Occasional teamwork is exhibited.*

_____Occasionally (several times a grading period), assess websites based on the criteria in *Figure 31* (full size assessment at end of lesson):

Figure 31—Student website rubric

Evaluation scale:

Exemplary:	32-36 points
Proficient:	28-31 points
Partially Proficient or Incomplete:	< 28 points (resubmit)

CRITERIA	Exemplary	Proficient	Partially	Incomplete	POINTS
Relevance of Content to Students and Parents	**9 points** • Content has useful information • Content is clear, concise; points readers to up to date resources. • Content is updated frequently	**6 points** • Content points readers to quality resources, is informative • Resources are clearly described so readers can navigate easily	**3 points** • Content points to unrelated information. • Resources are not clearly described so readers cannot navigate easily.	**0 points** • Resources pointed to are inaccurate, misleading or inappropriate • Annotations are missing, do not describe what is found	
Use of Media	**6 points** • Media enhance content and interest. • Creativity enhances content	**4 points** • Most media enhance content. • Most files show creativity	**2 points** • Some media don't enhance content. • Some use of creativity is evident to enhance content.	**0 points** • Media are inappropriate or detract from content.	
Fair Use Guidelines	**6 points** Fair use guidelines are followed with proper citations.	**4 points** Fair use guidelines are frequently followed; most material is cited.	**2 points** Sometimes fair use guidelines are followed with some citations.	**0 points** Fair use guidelines are not followed. Material is improperly cited.	
Links	**3 points** All links are active and functioning.	**2 points** Most links are active	**1 point** Some links are not active.	**0 points** Many links are not active.	
Layout and Text Elements	**3 points** • Fonts are easy-to-read • Use of bullets, italics, bold, enhances readability. • Consistent format throughout	**2 points** • Sometimes fonts, size, bullets, italics, bold, detract from readability. • Minor formatting inconsistencies exist	**1 point** • Text is difficult to read due to formatting	**0 points** • Text is difficult to read with misuse of fonts, size, bullets, italics, bold • Many formatting tools are misused	
Writing Mechanics	**3 points** No grammar, capitalization, punctuation, spelling errors	**2 points** Few grammar, capitalization, punctuation, and spelling errors	**1 point** 4+ errors in grammar, capitalization, punctuation, and spelling	**0 points** More than 6 grammar/ spelling/ punctuation errors.	
				TOTAL POINTS	/30

Study Helper

_____ Study Helpers are online tools that assist students in test preparation, such as (search internet for websites):

- *Jeopardy Labs_Jeopardy format*
- *Puzzle maker*
- *Rubrics*
- *Study Blue_to make flash cards*
- *Rubrics/Assessments—long list of resources from Kathy Schrock*

_____Require these occasionally throughout the year so students are familiar with the concept, comfortable with use, and able to employ them to achieve educational goals.

Video Channel

_____This is a class video channel on YouTube, Vimeo, TeacherTube or SchoolTube where teacher summaries, homework videos, and how-tos are posted.
_____Show students how to set channel to 'private'.
_____Videos can be embedded into blogs, websites, wiki pages, digital portfolios.

Virtual Meeting Rooms

_____Students meet each other or the teacher to discuss class activities outside of class time. This can be a study group, tutoring, or a group to prepare a class project.
_____Popular tools are Google Meet, Zoom, and Teams (Google for addresses) or another tool that allows students to meet online in real-time.
_____Depending upon your school, you may require parent permission slips.

Vocabulary Decoding Tools

_____Show students how to access the native apps or webtools on their digital devices that decode vocabulary students don't understand. Depending upon the device, these will be on the device homepage, browser toolbar, a shortkey, or a right click. Show students how to quickly look up words from any class rather than skip over content that includes the word. Let them practice with several of the words in this lesson's *Vocabulary* list.
_____Options include:

- *right click on word in MS Word and select 'Look up'*
- *right click in Google Apps (i.e., Google Docs) and select 'research'*
- *use an online resource like Dictionary.com*
- *use a browser app or plug-in*

Summatively

_____Students work in groups to become familiar with digital tools. When (or as) they review a tool, expect them to:

- *blog and comment on other blogs*
- *set up groups in Google Apps*
- *participate in an out-of-school virtual meeting to share materials, teach each other how to do skills, and share thoughts on the class digital tools*
- *collect online tool links to a central location like their blog sidebar*
- *check in on class Twitter feed sharing how far they are, questions, ideas, using topic #hashtags*

      • *create a homework drop box and share at least one doc with the teacher*
      • *create a group folder and share information with group members*

_____Have student groups create a slideshow, Prezi, or another communication tool (think back to tools used in seventh grade) answering questions about one or more digital tools: 1) what is it, 2) what do I use it for, and 3) what are the pros and cons.

_____A note: Every chance you get, use technology to facilitate teaching. Lead by example. Students will see you use tech quickly and facilely and follow your good example. They want to use tech. Don't discourage them!

Class exit ticket: ***Students send a well-constructed email, tweet, or comment to a classmate and reply to one they receive appropriately.***

Differentiation

- *Explore inside computer.*
- *Check YouTube for discussion on using Padlet.*
- *Create a Voki as an introduction to student wiki or blog.*
- *Create a Tagxedo on what students think about technology, what tools they're excited to learn, or a profile of themselves. Share on wiki, Site, or blog.*
- *Students who finish can start homework preview of next unit posted to class website, wiki, Google Drive—wherever works best for your class community.*

Assessment 1—Parts of the computer

HARDWARE—PARTS OF THE COMPUTER

Student name: _____

Name each part of computer hardware system and whether it's INPUT or OUTPUT.
Spelling must be correct to get credit

1 _____

2 _____

4 _____

3 _____

5 _____

6 _____

7 _____

HARDWARE—PARTS OF THE SMARTPHONE

Adapt this to your needs

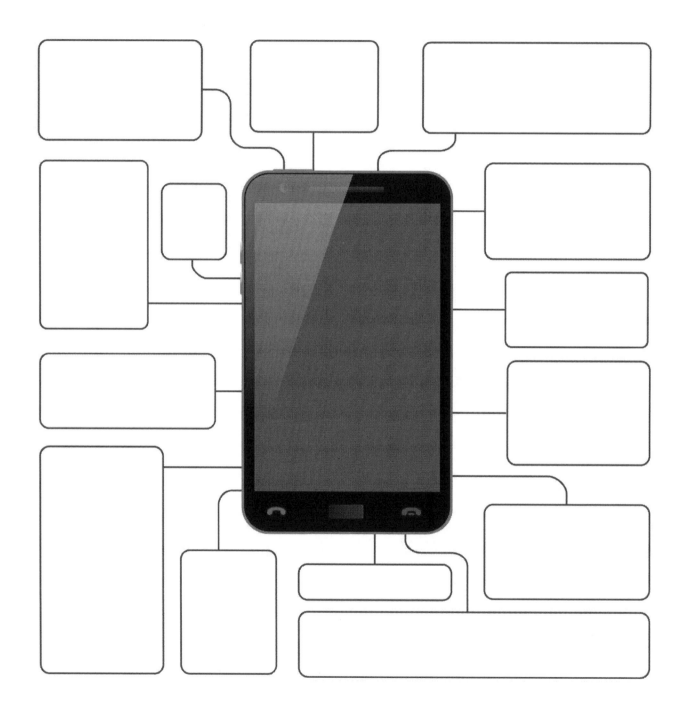

Parts of an iPad

©AskATechTeacher

Assessment 4—Chromebook parts

Parts of a Chromebook

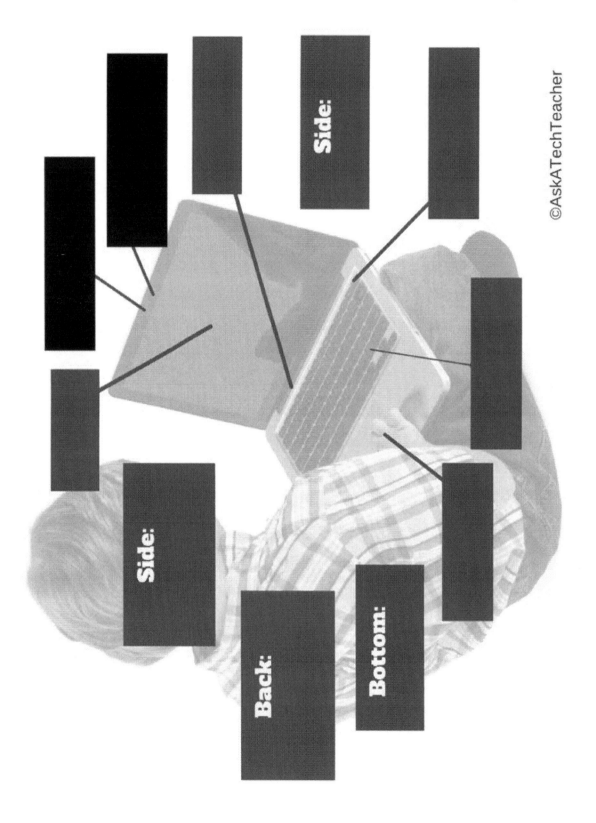

©AskATechTeacher

Assessment 5—Student blogging agreement

Eighth Grade Blogging Rules

1. I will not give out any information more personal than my first name
2. I will not plagiarize; instead I will expand on others' ideas and give credit where it is due.
3. I will use language appropriate for school.
4. I will always respect my fellow students and their writing.
5. I will only post pieces that I am comfortable with everyone seeing.
6. I will use constructive/productive/purposeful criticism, supporting any idea, comment, or critique I have with evidence.
7. I will take blogging seriously, posting only comments and ideas that are meaningful and that contribute to the overall conversation.
8. I will take my time when I write, using formal language (not text lingo), and I will try to spell everything correctly.
9. I will not bully others in my blog posts or in my comments.
10. I will only post comments on posts that I have fully read, rather than just skimmed.
11. I will not reveal anyone else's identity in my comments or posts.

Any infraction of the Blogging Rules may result in loss of blogging privileges and an alternative assignment will be required.

Student Signature _____ Date _____

Assessment 6—Blog grading rubric

Student Blog Rubric

Adapted from University of Wisconsin-Stout

Exemplary: 32-36 points
Proficient: 28-31 points
Partially Proficient or Incomplete: < 28 points (resubmit)

CRITERIA	Exemplary	Proficient	Partial	Incomplete	POINTS
Relevance of Content to Students and Parents	**9 points** • Content has useful information • Content is clear, concise; points readers to up to date resources. • Blog is updated frequently	**6 points** • Content points readers to quality resources, is informative • Resources are clearly described so readers can navigate easily	**3 points** • Content points to unrelated information. • Resources are not clearly described so readers cannot navigate easily.	**0 points** • Resources pointed to are inaccurate, misleading or inappropriate • Annotations are missing, do not describe what is found	
Use of Media	**6 points** • Media enhance content and interest. • Creativity enhances content	**4 points** • Most media enhance content. • Most files show creativity	**2 points** • Some media don't enhance content. • Some use of creativity is evident to enhance content.	**0 points** • Media are inappropriate or detract from content.	
Fair Use Guidelines	**6 points** Fair use guidelines are followed with proper citations.	**4 points** Fair use guidelines are frequently followed; most material is cited.	**2 points** Sometimes fair use guidelines are followed with some citations.	**0 points** Fair use guidelines are not followed. Material is improperly cited.	
Links	**3 points** All links are active and functioning.	**2 points** Most links are active	**1 point** Some links are not active.	**0 points** Many links are not active.	
Layout and Text Elements	**3 points** • Fonts are easy-to-read • Use of bullets, italics, bold, enhances readability. • Consistent format throughout	**2 points** • Sometimes fonts, size, bullets, italics, bold, detract from readability. • Minor formatting inconsistencies exist	**1 point** • Text is difficult to read due to formatting	**0 points** • Text is difficult to read with misuse of fonts, size, bullets, italics, bold • Many formatting tools are misused	
Writing Mechanics	**3 points** No grammar, capitalization, punctuation, spelling errors	**2 points** Few grammar, capitalization, punctuation, and spelling errors	**1 point** 4+ errors in grammar, capitalization, punctuation, and spelling	**0 points** More than 6 grammar/ spelling/ punctuation errors.	
				TOTAL POINTS	/30

Assessment 7—Website grading rubric

Student Website Rubric

Adapted from University of Wisconsin-Stout

Evaluation scale:

Exemplary:	32-36 points
Proficient:	28-31 points
Partially Proficient or Incomplete:	< 28 points (resubmit)

CRITERIA	Exemplary	Proficient	Partially	Incomplete	POINTS
Relevance of Content to Students and Parents	**9 points** • Content has useful information • Content is clear, concise; points readers to up to date resources. • Content is updated frequently	**6 points** • Content points readers to quality resources, is informative • Resources are clearly described so readers can navigate easily	**3 points** • Content points to unrelated information. • Resources are not clearly described so readers cannot navigate easily.	**0 points** • Resources pointed to are inaccurate, misleading or inappropriate • Annotations are missing, do not describe what is found	
Use of Media	**6 points** • Media enhance content and interest. • Creativity enhances content	**4 points** • Most media enhance content. • Most files show creativity	**2 points** • Some media don't enhance content. • Some use of creativity is evident to enhance content.	**0 points** • Media are inappropriate or detract from content.	
Fair Use Guidelines	**6 points** Fair use guidelines are followed with proper citations.	**4 points** Fair use guidelines are frequently followed; most material is cited.	**2 points** Sometimes fair use guidelines are followed with some citations.	**0 points** Fair use guidelines are not followed. Material is improperly cited.	
Links	**3 points** All links are active and functioning.	**2 points** Most links are active	**1 point** Some links are not active.	**0 points** Many links are not active.	
Layout and Text Elements	**3 points** • Fonts are easy-to-read • Bullets, italics, bold, enhances readability. • Consistent format throughout	**2 points** • Sometimes fonts, size, bullets, italics, bold, detract from readability. • Minor formatting inconsistencies exist	**1 point** • Text is difficult to read due to formatting	**0 points** • Text is difficult to read with misuse of fonts, size, bullets, italics, bold • Many formatting tools are misused	
Writing Mechanics	**3 points** No grammar, capitalization, punctuation, spelling errors	**2 points** Few grammar, capitalization, punctuation, and spelling errors	**1 point** 4+ errors in grammar, capitalization, punctuation, and spelling	**0 points** More than 6 grammar/ spelling/ punctuation errors.	
				TOTAL POINTS	/30

Assessment 8—Digital portfolio rubric

Digital Portfolio Rubric

CATEGORY	Exemplary	Proficient	Developing	Unsatisfactory	RATING
Selection of Artifacts	All artifacts and work samples are clearly and directly related to the purpose of portfolio.	Most artifacts and work samples are related to the purpose of the digital portfolio.	Some of the artifacts and work samples are related to the purpose of the digital portfolio.	None of the artifacts and work samples is related to the purpose of portfolio.	
Reflections	All reflections clearly describe growth, achievement and accomplishments, and include goals for continued learning (long and short term).	Most reflections describe growth and include goals for continued learning. It is clear student put thought and consideration into writing.	A few of the reflections describe growth and include goals for continued learning. It is not clear student put thought into his/her writing.	None of the reflections describe growth and does not include goals for continued learning. It is clear student put little thought into these writings.	
Use of Multimedia	Photographs, graphics, audio and/or video files enhance concepts, ideas and relationships, create interest, and are appropriate for chosen purpose.	Most graphic elements and multimedia contribute to concepts, ideas and relationships, enhance the written material and create interest.	Some of the graphic elements and multimedia do not contribute to concepts, ideas and relationships.	Multimedia doesn't contribute to concepts, ideas and relationships. The inappropriate use of multimedia detracts from content.	
Documentation & Copyright	All images, media and text follow copyright guidelines with accurate citations. All content throughout portfolio displays appropriate copyright permissions.	Most images, media and text created by others are cited with accurate, properly formatted citations.	Some images, media or text created by others are not cited with accurate, properly formatted citations.	No images, media or text created by others are cited with accurate, properly formatted citations.	
Ease of Navigation	Navigation links are intuitive. The various parts of portfolio are labeled, clearly organized and allow reader to easily locate an artifact.	Navigation links generally function well, but it is not always clear how to locate an artifact or move to related pages or different section.	Navigation links are confusing and it is often unclear how to locate an artifact or move to related pages or section.	Navigation links are confusing, and it is difficult to locate artifacts and move to related pages or a different section.	
Layout and Text Elements	Digital portfolio is easy to read. Fonts and type size vary appropriately for headings, sub-headings and text. Use of font styles (italic, bold, underline) is consistent and improves readability.	Digital portfolio is generally easy to read. Fonts and type size vary appropriately for headings, sub-headings and text. Use of font styles (italic, bold, underline) is generally consistent.	Digital portfolio is often difficult to read due to inappropriate use of fonts and type size for headings, sub-headings and text or inconsistent use of font styles (italic, bold, underline).	Digital portfolio is difficult to read due to inappropriate use of fonts, type size for headings, subheadings and text, and font styles (italic, bold, underline).	
Captions	All artifacts are accompanied by a caption that clearly explains importance of item including title, author, and date.	Most artifacts are accompanied by a caption that clearly explains importance of item including title, author, and date.	Some artifacts are accompanied by caption that explains importance of item including title, author, and date.	No artifacts are accompanied by a caption that explains importance of item.	
Writing Mechanics	There are no errors in grammar, capitalization, punctuation, and spelling.	There are few errors in grammar and spelling. These require minor editing and revision.	There are four or more errors in grammar and spelling requiring editing and revision.	There are more than six errors in grammar and spelling requiring major editing and revision.	

Article 9—Which Class Internet Start Page is Best

Which Class Internet Start Page is Best?

The Internet is unavoidable in education. Students go there to research, access homework, check grades, and a whole lot more. As a teacher, you do your best to make it a friendly, intuitive, and safe place to visit, but it's challenging. Students arrive there by iPads, smartphones, links from classroom teachers, suggestions from friends—the routes are endless. The best way to keep the Internet experience safe is to catch users right at the front door, on that first click.

How do you do that? By creating a **class Internet start page**. Clicking the Internet icon opens the World Wide Web to a default page. Never take your device's default because there's no guarantee it's G-rated enough for a typical classroom environment. Through the 'settings' function on your browser, enter the address of a page you've designed as a portal to all school Internet activity, called an 'Internet start page'. Sure, this takes some time to set-up and maintain, but it saves more than that in student frustration, lesson prep time, and the angst parents feel about their children entering the virtual world by themselves. They aren't. You're there, through this page. Parents can save the link to their home computer and let students access any resources on it, with the confidence of knowing you've curated everything.

In searching for the perfect Internet start page, I wanted one that:

- *quickly differentiates for different grades*
- *is intuitive for even the youngest to find their page*
- *is customizable across tabbed pages to satisfy changing needs*
- *presents a visual and playful interface to make students want to go there rather than find work-arounds (a favorite hobby of older students)*
- *includes an immediately visible calendar of events*
- *hosts videos of class events*
- *provides collaborative walls like Padlet*
- *includes other interactive widgets to excite students about technology*

Here are some I looked at:

Symbaloo

A logo-based website curation tool with surprising flexibility in how links are collected and displayed. It's hugely popular with educators because collections are highly-visual and easy to access and use. Plus, Symbaloo collections made by one teacher can be shared with the community, making link collections that much easier to curate.

The downside: Links are about all you can collect on Symbaloo.

Ustart

Offers a good collection of useful webtools for students including links, news, calendar, notes, even weather. It provides tabs for arranging themed collections (like classes) and is intuitive to set up and use. It even includes options for embeddable widgets like Padlet. This is the closest to what I needed of all three.

Overall: This is a good alternative to the one I selected.

Protopage

Protopage did everything on my list. It's flexible, customizable, intuitive, and quick to use with a scalable interface that can be adjusted to my needs (2-5 columns, resize boxes, drag widgets between tabs—that sort). I set up a separate tab for each grade (or you can set up tabs for subjects). The amount of tabs is limited only by space on the top toolbar. Resources included on each tab can be curated exactly as you need. Mine includes:

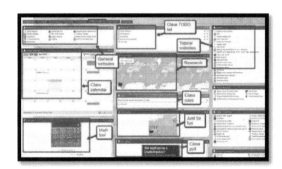

- *oft-used websites*
- *themed collections of websites*
- *a To Do list*
- *an interactive map*
- *a calculator*
- *a calendar of events*

- *edit-in-place sticky notes*
- *pictures of interest*
- *rss feeds of interest*
- *weather*
- *news*
- *widget for polling the class (Padlet)*

In addition, the Protopage folks are helpful. Whenever I have a problem (which is rare), they fix it quickly.

Article 10—13 Ways Blogs Teach Common Core

13 Ways Blogs Teach Common Core

If you aren't blogging with your students, you're missing one of the most effective tools available for improving student literacy and math. Blogs are easy to use, fun for students, encourage creativity and problem-solving, allow for reflection and feedback, enable publishing and sharing of work, and fulfill many of the Common Core Standards you might be struggling to complete. Aside from math and literacy, Common Core wants students to become accomplished in a variety of intangible skills that promote learning and college and career readiness. Look at these 13 benefits of blogging and how they align with Common Core:

1. **Provide and get feedbac**k—building a community via comments is an integral part of blogging. If you didn't want feedback, you'd publish a white paper or submit work the old fashioned hard copy way. When students publish their ideas in blogs, other students, teachers, parents can provide feedback, join the conversation, and learn from the student.

2. **Write-edit-review-rewrite**—teachers don't expect students to get it right the first time. Part of the writing process is revising, editing, rewriting. This is easy with blogs. Students publish a topic, collect comments, incorporate these ideas into their own thinking, and then edit their post.

3. **Publish**—the idea that student work is created for a grade then stuffed away in a corner of their closet is disappearing. Current educators want students to publish their work in a way that allows everyone to benefit from the student's knowledge and work. There are many ways to do that—blogs are one of the easiest.

4. **Share**—just like publishing, students no longer create for a grade; they share with others. Blogs allow for sharing of not only writing, but artwork, photography, music, multimedia projects, pretty much anything the student can create.

5. **Collaborate**—blogs can easily be collaborative. Student groups can publish articles, comment on others, edit and rewrite. They can work together on one blog to cover a wider variety of topics and/or make its design attractive, appealing and enticing to readers.

6. **Keyboarding**—blogs are small doses of typing—300-500 words, a few dozen for comments. This is an authentic opportunity to practice the keyboarding skills students will need for Common Core Standards in 4th grade and up.

7. **Demonstrate independence**—blogs are about creativity. No two are alike. They offer lots of options for design and formatting so students can tweak it to their preference. Because they are open 24/7, students can do blog work when it suits them, not in the confines of a 50-minute class.

8. **Build strong content knowledge**—blog posts can be drafted as the student collects information, posted when the student is ready. Links can be included to provide evidence of student statements, as well as linkbacks for reference and deeper reading for interested students.

9. **respond to the varying demands of audience, task, purpose, and discipline**—Students can create their work in whatever digital tool fits the audience, task, purpose they are focused on, and then embed it into their blog post. This is possible even in a simplified blogging platform like Kidblog. Most

online tools (such as Voki, Wordle, and Tagxedo) provide the html codes that can be easily placed in the blog post. Then, the student at their option can focus on presenting their ideas as music, art, photos, text, an infographic, a word cloud—whatever works for their purposes.

10. **Comprehend as well as critique**—student bloggers are expected to critique the posts of others by thoroughly reading the post and commenting based on evidence. If the reader doesn't understand, they ask questions in the comments. This insures that when they evaluate the post, they have all the information required to reach a conclusion.

11. **Value evidence**—blogs make it easy to provide all the necessary evidence to support a point of view. Students can link back to sources to provide credit and link to experts to provide credibility for statements. In fact, in the blogosphere, good bloggers are expected to do this as a means of building credibility for opinions they write

12. **Use technology and digital media strategically and capably**—certainly blogs are great for writing, but they're also excellent as digital portfolios to display student work developed in a variety of places. Students pick the technology that fits what they're expected to accomplish in a class, then publish it to the blog. Have you seen the movies students put together on a topic? Some are amazing.

13. **Understand other perspectives and cultures**—blogs are published to the Internet. Even private blogs are accessed by many more people than possible with a hand-written paper. Students write knowing that people of all cultures and perspectives will read their material, knowing they can add comments that share their beliefs. This encourages students to develop the habit of thinking about *perspective* as they write.

Don't try all of this at once. Spiral into it, starting in second or third grade. Let their blogging grow with their intellectual skills.

Article 11—How to integrate Web Tools into the Classroom

How to Integrate Web Tools into the Classroom

'**Web 2.0**' is a term familiar to all teachers. Stated in its simplest form, it's the set of interactive internet-based tools used by students to enrich educational opportunities—blogs, wikis, class internet homepages, class internet start pages, twitter, social bookmarks, podcasting, photo sharing, online docs, online calendars, even Second Life—tools that require thoughtful interaction between the student and the site. For teachers, it's a challenge to keep up with the plethora of options as the creative minds of our new adults stretch the boundaries of what

we can do on the internet. Students, adults, teachers who use this worldwide wealth of information and tools are referred to as 'digital citizens'. They leave a vast digital footprint and it is incumbent upon them to make healthy and safe decisions, including:

- *Treat others and their property with respect (for example, plagiarism—even undiscovered—is immoral and illegal)*
- *Act in a responsible manner*
- *Look after their own security*

Here are some activities you can do in your classroom that will make your lessons and activities more student-centered and more relevant to this new generation of students:

1. Create a **classroom blog**. Blogging has become one of the most effective learning tools in education. It introduces students to new methods of communicating, improves their writing, and motivates them to find their voice. You ask students about it, they'll tell you—blogs make learning fun.

2. Create a **classroom internet start page.** When students log onto the internet, have them bring up a start page with information relevant to them—targeted links, a To Do list, RSS feeds, search tools, email. Ask them what should be on it. Maybe they'd like sponge websites to fill extra minutes. Make it exciting!

3. Each has a library of custom fields to individualize the start-up experience.

4. Build your own **classroom webpage**. Make it a learning portal open for business 24/7. Make sure it engages students while facilitating authentic real-world activities.

5. Create **online calendars** for students. These replace the traditional planners students carry to classes (and lose who knows where which becomes a traumatic event in young lives). Create your own on Google Calendars with viewing privileges for students and parents only, and then embed it into your class webpage, start page or wiki.

6. Create a **wiki**—a web page built by and for students. The most famous example is Wikipedia. Wikis can communicate school news, information on a research topic, terminology—whatever you want. For example, after teaching a lesson, have students go to the class wiki and summarize what they understood. Then, when test time arrives, students can study from everyone's notes.

7. Set up **social bookmarking** so students can save links to webpages they use for research, sports, music, and share them with others. Imagine the vast database you can compile by having students investigate a topic—say, the French Revolution—save the sites they visit to a group folder, and benefit from each other's research. What an amazing tool!

8. **Twitter** is a free social messaging utility that allows you to update parents and older students via short messages everyone will have time to read. In my case, I have one account for parents (it's private, so I won't share it here) and one for my PLN (personal learning network—I'd love to have you follow me). You can incorporate twitter widgets into webpages, add it to your Google desktop/ smartphone/ iPad, even your blog.

9. **Photo sharing** through Flickr or Photobucket (or others). Free online photo collections enable students/parents/teachers to share pictures from school events, sports and more. Students can search for photos to help with research (be sure to teach them correct annotations) and educators can upload photos for classes, school events, and more. At my school, students had to complete a photo journal after a field trip. Everyone uploaded their pictures, creating a huge pool to use for the follow-up project.

10. **Podcasting** is an efficient method of sharing lectures, instructions, and information. They appeal to those multi-intelligences that prefer visual and audio and can be replayed 24/7. With a nominal amount of equipment, anyone can create files and post them to the internet that can be accessed from a personal computer or handheld device. The most popular site is YouTube, but also try Vimeo.

11. Everyone should try **online docs.** Google Docs has become the standard for free, easy-to-use document sharing at schools and can be limited to the school community of registered users. Even if you don't use it in your school, share it with parents. You'll be surprised how many will appreciate the alternative to MS Office.

Which others do you use to enhance and enrich your school teaching?
Photo credit: Johns Hopkins School of Education

Article 12—8 Things My Blog Taught Me

8 Things My Blog Taught Me

When I started blogging, I wasn't sure where to take it. I knew I wanted to connect with other tech teachers so I used that as the theme. Now, thanks to the 491,000+ people who have visited, I know much more about the 'why'. It's about getting to know kindred souls, but there is so much more I've gotten from blogging. Like these:

How to write

I've learned to be frugal with my words. I choose verbiage that conveys more than one-word's-worth of information and I leave tangential issues for another post. Because I realize readers are consuming on the run, I make sure to be clear–no misplaced pronouns or fuzzy concepts like 'thing' or 'something'.

Prove my point

This part of writing transcends what print journalists must do. Yes, they do it, but my readers expect me to support ideas with interactive links to sources. If I'm reviewing a tech ed concept, I link to other websites for deeper reading. That's something that can't happen in paper writing. Sure, they can provide the link, but to put the paper down, open the laptop, copy that link–I mean, who does that? In a blog, I get annoyed if someone cites research and doesn't provide the link.

Listen

When I write an article, I cross post to other parts of my PLN, sometimes to ezines I contribute to in other parts of the world. And then I listen. What are readers saying? What are their comments/suggestions to me? Often, I learn as much from readers as what I thought I knew when I wrote the article.

How to market my writing

I try lots of ideas to market my writing, but thanks to the blogosphere, I know what everyone else is doing. I can try as much or little of it as I want. For me, I found a comfortable baseline and add a few pieces every year (this year, it's Pinterest).

One point worth mentioning is headlines. Usually, all I get from a reader is seven seconds–long enough to read the title, maybe the first line. If my title doesn't seem personal and relevant, potential readers move on. There are over 450 million English language blogs. That's a lot of competition. I better hit a home run with the title.

There are lots of opinions out there

Often, I share my thoughts on the future or current status of tech ed. Sometimes, I'm surprised at comments I get. They might touch a corner of the idea I hadn't thought of or be 180 degrees from my conclusions. It forces me to think bigger as I write, consider how people who aren't me will read my words. That's both humbling and empowering. I think I'm much better at that than I used to be.

There are a lot of smart people in the world

In a previous lifetime when I built child care centers for a living, I read lots of data that said people thought the education system was broken–but not in their area. They considered themselves lucky because their schools worked. Well, as I meandered through life, I realized that applies to everything. People are happy with what they're comfortable with and frightened/suspicious of what they aren't used to. Through blogging, I get to delve into those ideas with them because we feel like friends. I've found that lots of people are smart, intuitive, engaged in life, looking to improve the world. I'm glad I learned that.

How to be responsible

Yes, blogging is demanding. I have to follow through on promises made in my blog profile and posts. When I say I'll offer tech tips weekly, I have to do that even if I'm tired or busy with other parts of my life. It's not as hard as it sounded when I first started. If you're a mom, you've got the mindset. Just apply it to blogging.

How to be a friend

My readers visit my posts and comment or poke me with a 'like'. Maybe, on my good days, they repost. Those are nice attaboys. I always return the favor by dropping by their blogs to see what they're up to, leave a comment on their latest article. It takes time, but like any relationship, is worth it. I have online friends I've never met who I feel closer to than half the people in my physical world. I've seen them struggle with cancer, new jobs, unemployment, kid problems. I've learned a lot about life from them.

Article 13—12 Ways Twitter Improves Education

12 Ways Twitter Improves Education

Twitter can easily be dismissed as a waste of time in the elementary school classroom. Students will get distracted. Students will see tweets they shouldn't at their age. How does one manage a room full of Tweeple without cell phones? Is it even appropriate for the lower grades?

Here's ammunition for what often turns into a pitched verbal brawl as well-intended teachers try to reach a compromise on Twitter (in fact, many of the new Web 2.0 tools—blogs, wikis, websites that require registrations and log-ins, discussion forums. You can probably add to this list) that works for all stakeholders:

You learn to be concise.

Twitter gives you only 280 characters to get the entire message across. *Letters, numbers, symbols, punctuation and spaces all count as characters on Twitter.* Wordiness doesn't work. Twitter counts every keystroke and won't publish anything with a minus in front of the word count.

At first blush, that seems impossible. It's not. True, you must know the right word for every situation. People with a big vocabulary are at an advantage because they don't use collections of little words to say what they mean, they jump right to it. All those hints your English teacher gave you–picture nouns and action verbs, get rid of adverbs and adjectives–take on new meaning to the Twitter aficionado.

Twitter isn't intimidating

A blank white page that holds hundreds of words, demanding you fill in each line margin to margin is intimidating. 280 characters aren't. Anyone can write 280 characters about any topic. Students write their 280 characters and more, learn to whittle back, leave out emotional words, adjectives and adverbs, pick better nouns and verbs because they need the room. Instead of worrying what they'll say on all those empty lines, they feel successful.

Students learn manners

Social networks are all about netiquette. People thank others for their assistance, ask politely for help, and encourage contributions from others. Use this framework to teach students how to engage in a community—be it physical or virtual. It's all about manners.

Students learn to be focused

With only 280 characters, you can't get off topic. You have to save those for a different tweet. Tweeple like that trait in writers. They like to hear what your main topic is and hear your thoughts on it, not your meanderings. When you force yourself to write this way, you find it really doesn't take a paragraph to make a point. Use the right words, people get it. Consider that the average reader gives a story seven seconds before moving on. OK, yes, that's more than 280 characters, but not much.

Here's an idea. If you feel you must get into those off-topic thoughts, write them in a separate tweet.

Students learn to share

Start a tweet stream where students share research websites on a topic. Maybe the class is studying Ancient Greece. Have each student share their favorite website (using a #hashtag — maybe #ancientgreece) and create a resource others can use. Expand on that wonderful skill they learned in kindergarten about sharing their toys with others. Encourage them to RT posts that they found particularly relevant or helpful.

Writing short messages perfects the art of "headlining".

Writers call this the title. Bloggers and journalists call it the headline. Whatever the label, it has to be cogent and pithy enough to pull the audience in and make them read the article. That's a tweet.

Tweets need to be written knowing that tweeple can @reply

Yes. This is the world of social networks where people will read what you say and comment. That's a good thing. It's feedback and builds an online community, be it for socializing or school. Students learn to construct their arguments expecting others to respond, question, and comment. Not only does this develop the skill of persuasive writing, students learn to have a thick skin, take comments with a grain of salt and two grains of aspirin.

#Hashmarks develop a community

Create #hashmarks to help students organize tweets: #help for a question, #homework for homework help. Establish class ones to deal with subjects that you as the teacher want students to address.

Students learn tolerance for all opinions

Why? Because Tweeple aren't afraid to voice their thoughts. They only have 280 characters—why not spit it right out. Because the Twitter stream is a public forum (in a classroom, the stream can be private, but still visible to all members of the class), students understand what they say is out there forever. That's daunting. Take the opportunity to teach students about their public profile. Represent themselves well with good grammar, good spelling, and well-chosen tolerant ideas. Don't be emotional or spiteful because it can't be taken back. Rather than shying away from exposing students to the world at large, use Twitter to teach students how to live in a world.

Students are engaged

Twitter is exciting, new, and hip. Students want to use it. It's not the boring worksheet. It's a way to engage students in ways that excite them.

Consider this: You're doing the lecture part of your teaching (we all have some of that), or you're walking the classroom helping where needed. Students can tweet questions that show up on the Smartboard. It's easy to see where everyone is getting stuck, which question is stumping them, and answer it in real time. The class barely slows down. Not only can you see where problems arise, students can provide instant feedback on material without disrupting the class. Three people can tweet at once while you talk/help.

Twitter, the Classroom Notepad

I tried this out after I read about it and turns out, it works as well for 8th graders as it does for higher education. Springboarding off student engagement, Twitter can act as your classroom notepad. Have students enter their thoughts, note, and reactions while you talk. By the time class is done, the entire class has an overview of the conversation with extensions and connections that help everyone get more out of the time spent together.

Twitter is always open

Inspiration doesn't always strike in that 50-minute class period. Sometimes it's after class, after school, after dinner, even 11 at night. Twitter doesn't care. Whatever schedule is best for students to discover the answer, Twitter is there. If you post a tweet question and ask students to join the conversation, they will respond in the time frame that works best for them. I love that. That's a new set of rules for classroom participation, and these are student-centered, uninhibited by a subjective time period. Twitter doesn't even care if a student missed the class. S/he can catch up via tweets and then join in.

Lesson #3 Keyboarding

Vocabulary	Problem solving	Homework
• Cumulative • Home row • Hunt-and-peck • Keyboard shortcuts • Mulligan • QWERTY • Shortkey • Tilde • Touch typing • Wpm	• I can't remember key placement (trust yourself to know) • Can't remember some keys (skip them) • I can't type with hands covered (Keep practicing) • Can't type faster (slow down, relax) • I keep losing home row (find bump on F and J with pointers) • I do fine with 2-4 fingers (but you won't get fast)	Keyboard 45 min, 15 minutes a time Review KB checklist and quiz Know 5 shortkeys Bring questions to class
Academic Applications Writing, research, any topic requiring keyboarding	**Required skills** Familiarity with touch typing, tech problem solving, speaking/listening skills, PDF annotation	**Standards** CCSS: W.8.6 NETS: 1d, 6a

Essential Question

How does technology make my work faster and more efficient?

Big Idea

Work on essential elements of keyboarding—technique, speed, and accuracy—with grade level goals

Teacher Preparation/Materials Required

- Have lesson preview materials online.
- Have student workbooks (if using).
- Integrate domain-specific tech vocabulary into lesson.
- Ensure all required links are on student digital devices.
- Have speed quiz, word processing program, blank keyboard quizzes, and handwriting quiz (as needed)
- Have keyboard programs, software and online.
- Know which tasks weren't completed last week.
- Something happen you weren't prepared for? Show students how you fix the emergency without a meltdown and with a positive attitude.

Assessment Strategies

- Previewed required material; came to class prepared
- Annotated workbook (if using)
- Worked independently
- Used good keyboarding habits
- Completing required quizzes
- Completed Challenge
- Completed Handwriting vs KB
- Completed formative projects
- Completed warm-up
- Joined classroom conversations
- [tried to] solve own problems
- Decisions followed class rules
- Left room as s/he found it
- Higher order thinking: analysis, evaluation, synthesis
- Habits of mind observed

Steps

Time required: *Spread throughout the school year with time set aside for quizzes*

Class warm-up: *Keyboarding on the class typing program, paying attention to hand placement, posture, and touch typing*

This lesson is spread throughout the year.

_____**Homework is assigned before class so students are prepared for class projects**

_____Any questions from preparatory homework?

_____Use backchannel program like Socrative to determine student understanding and where you might offer assistance.

_____Using *Figure 32 (*full size in Appendix*)*, discuss why students should care about keyboarding:

Figure 32—Why learn to keyboard

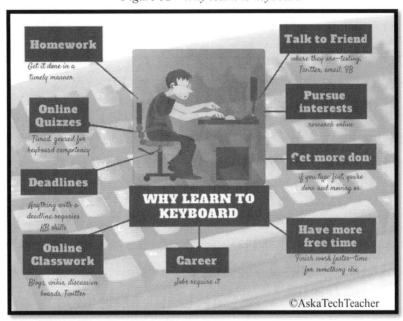

_____At this point in student keyboarding development, they should:

- ○ *keep copy to the side of the keyboard*
- ○ *use correct posture—legs in front, body in front and one hand's width from the table, elbows at your sides, posture upright, feet flat on floor, hands curled over home row*
- ○ *take proper care of tech equipment*
- ○ *effectively use software and internet-based sites for keyboard practice*

_____Have students check the posture of a neighbor. If correct posture isn't already a habit, encourage students to sit this way when they use a digital device—home, school, the library, everywhere (*Figures 33a-b*—zoom in if needed):

Figure 33a—Keyboarding posture; 33b—position

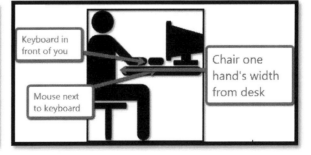

_____Review how student hands should look (*Figures 34a-b*):

Figure 34a-b—Keyboarding hand position

_____Keyboarding is cumulative. What can be learned depends heavily upon what was learned earlier. If hunt 'n peck becomes ingrained, it's difficult to develop competence later.

_____Review keyboarding best practices that you will observe as students work. *Figure 35* is a list. There's an assessment at end of Lesson:

Figure 35—Keyboarding technique checklist

Student _____

Keyboarding Technique Checklist
(3rd – Middle School Grades)

Technique	Date	Date	Date	Date	Date
Feet placed for balance and sits up straight.					
Body centered to the middle of keyboard.					
Eyes on the screen.					
Types with correct fingering.					
Types with a steady, even rhythm.					
Keeps fingers on home row keys.					
Has a good attitude and strives for improvement.					
WPM (words per minute)					
Accuracy percent					

4 pts = Mastery level 　　2 pts = Partial Mastery level
3 pts = Near Mastery level 　　1 pt = Minimal Mastery level

- *Keep hands curved over home row.*
- *Use correct posture:*

  o *Sit straight, shoulders back, head up, body centered one hand's width from the table, feet flat on the ground.*
  o *Keep elbows close to your sides.*
  o *Reach for keys—don't move hands (only fingers).*

- *Touch type with a steady, even pace.*
- *Keep copy to side of keyboard, eyes on copy or screen—NOT keyboard.*
- *Use keyboard shortcuts (i.e., Ctrl+B, Shift+Alt+D).*

_____If students just started to practice keyboarding, assess only a few criteria. As K-7th graders get more practice, they'll come to 8th grade with a greater facility and you can expect more of them.

_____Add each keyboarding activity to class calendar.

_____By the end of 8th grade, students should (see Scope and Sequence at end of unit):

- ○ *Touch type 45 wpm.*
- ○ *Type three pages in a single sitting.*
- ○ *Compose at keyboard with ease; keep eyes on copy.*
- ○ *Know at least twenty shortkeys (i.e., Alt+F4, Esc, Ctrl+P, Ctrl+S, Ctrl+C, Ctrl+V, Ctrl+Alt+Del, Ctrl+B/I/U, double-click to enlarge window, Alt+Tab, Win key, Shift+tab, right mouse button key, Ctrl+, Ctrl-, ???).*
- ○ *Reach fingers from home row to other keys. When viewed, hands should appear still with fingers moving—no flying hands.*
- ○ *Understand most common keys (see Important Keys assessment at end of Unit).*
- ○ *Be able to present thoughts in written format in a way that represents student well— good formatting, minimal errors, quickly.*
- ○ *Understand keyboard parts and functions.*
- ○ *Be able to present their thoughts in written format in a way that represents student well—good formatting, minimal errors, and quickly.*
- ○ *Understand keyboard parts and functions.*

Figure 36—Keyboarding basic

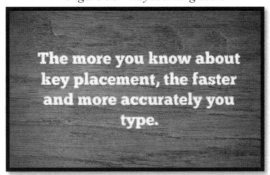

_____Use checklist at the end of the Unit to track student progress throughout the year.

_____Let students know **Mulligan Rule** applies for assessments (poster in Appendix). What's that? Any golfers? A 'mulligan' is a do-over. Students can retake any quiz/project/test covered by Mulligan Rule without losing credit. I love the Mulligan Rule. It covers those times students complain they weren't ready, didn't know about a quiz, were sick, shouldn't be graded because [fill in the blank]. I don't argue. I smile and let them retake it. Few do. It requires little from me, yet I seem like the world's fairest teacher.

_____Practice one keyboard row at a time. Here's a schedule for the **first six weeks**:

- *Weeks 1-2: home row*
- *Weeks 3-4: QWERTY row*
- *Weeks 5-6: lower row*

_____Enter these into class calendar.

_____Students practice 10-15 minutes during class and 45 minutes per week (15 minutes at a sitting) as homework.

_____**Throughout year**, observe students as they type and evaluate:

- *Causes of errors include tension, wandering attention, faulty reading, wrong mindset.*
- *Watch students for fatigue—moving heads, massaging, and tight facial expressions.*

_____For more, review article at the end of the lesson, *"How to Prepare for Year-end Tests".*

_____Here are eight activities included in this lesson, to be spread throughout the year:

- *authentic keyboarding using inquiry-based projects*
- *blank keyboard quiz*
- *formative assessments*
- *handwriting vs. keyboarding*
- *important keys quiz*
- *keyboarding challenge*
- *shortkeys*
- *summative speed/accuracy quizzes*

_____For more activities, read *"5 Ways to Make Keyboarding Fun"* at end of lesson.

Authentic keyboarding using inquiry-based projects

_____Typing is best learned through class inquiry. As soon as possible, begin project-based typing. These can be short reports, magazines, trifolds, a story—what works best for your students. *Figures 37a-e* are projects in the K-7 curriculum that reinforce authentic keyboarding:

Figure 37a-e—Project-based learning and keyboarding

_____With digital tool unit completed, expect students to do the following activities that reinforce both learning and keyboarding skills:

- *Blog weekly to reflect on current unit. Visit classmate blogs and join conversations.*
- *Use digital note-taking tools for notes.*
- *Use digital portfolio for storage of class materials.*
- *Submit all homework via a class dropbox.*
- *Participate in class Twitter account daily using appropriate #hashtags (if using this).*
- *Use student website as assigned by teacher.*

Shortkeys

_____Throughout year, reinforce the use of shortkeys. For example:

- *close a program—Alt+F4*
- *copy—Ctrl+C*
- *enter date—Shift+Alt+D*
- *indent—Tab and Shift+tab*
- *paste—Ctrl+V (why not Ctrl+P?)*
- *print—Ctrl+P*
- *save—Ctrl+S*
- *taskbar disappears—push Win key*
- *toggle between two window—Alt+Tab*
- *undo an action—Ctrl+Z*

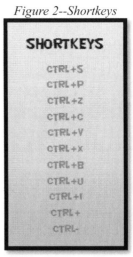

Figure 2--Shortkeys

_____If using workbooks, have students take a screenshot of *Figure 38*, print, and tape to their digital device or notebook.

_____See *Figures 39a-d* for platform-specific shortkeys (full-size posters in Appendix):

Figure 39a—iPad shortkeys; 39b—Chromebook shortkeys; 39c—PC shortkeys; 39d—Internet shortkeys

 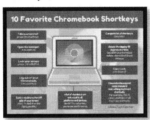  

Formative assessments

_____Once a month, practice on a site like TypingTest.com to see how fast/accurately students are typing. The goal is 45 wpm. If students get more than five errors, they should slow down; less than five, speed up.

_____Review keyboarding Scope and Sequence (at the end of this lesson) in preparation for today's assessment. Students reviewed this for homework. Do they have any questions? Anything that should be added?

Summative speed/accuracy quizzes

_____**Each grading period,** students test speed and accuracy to track improvement. The first quiz is a benchmark—to evaluate skills. The rest are graded based on improvement. If students do their homework and use good habits at the computer, they'll do fine.

- *20% improvement   10/10*
- *10-20% improvement 9/10*
- *1-10% improvement   8/10*

- *No improvement   7/10*
- *Slowed down   6/10*

_____Grade level standard: **45 wpm.** If students haven't practiced keyboarding for several years (or used this curriculum since kindergarten), adjust this to a speed more suited to their skillset.

_____The speed quiz can be delivered several ways:

- *Place a page from a book being read on the class screen. Students copy it for the quiz. This method forces their eyes up rather than on their hands.*
- *Print a page from a book being read in class. Students place it to the side of their keyboard and type from it.*
- *Use an online typing test like TypingTest.com.*

_____Students type for three-five minutes, then save/share/print.

_____Load a digital copy of *Assessment* at the end of this lesson onto your iPad and fill it in for each student with an annotation tool like Notability or Adobe Reader.

_____If students use the workbooks, have them record their score for later comparison.

Important Keys Quiz

_____Discuss why it's important that students memorize keys.

Figure 40—Important keys on keyboard

_____**Each grading period**, students take a blank Important Keys quiz (*Figure 40* and *Assessment* at end of Lesson—adapt to your digital device) to test key placement knowledge. They work in pairs and must retake until they pass. Success translates to speed and accuracy.

_____Pass out blank Important Keys quiz. Students get 10 minutes to complete.

_____If you are going to give this quiz more than once (say, once a grading period), use this first one as a baseline. Next time, students must improve. Score it like the keyboard speed quiz.

Blank keyboard quiz

_____**Each grading period**, students take a blank keyboard quiz (*Figures 41a-b* are blank keyboards for a PC and a Chromebook. Adapt as needed for your digital device. See end of Lesson for *Assessments*) to test knowledge of key placement. They can work in pairs and must retake until they pass.

_____Discuss why it's important that students memorize keys, how it translates to speed, accuracy, and facility with touch typing.

_____Students get ten minutes to complete. The first quiz is a baseline. Next time, quizzes are graded like keyboard speed quiz—on improvement.

_____Common mistakes are forgetting *Esc* at left side of F row, forgetting tilde at left side of number row, and getting QWERTY row wrong.

_____If students are using the workbooks, have them record their speed/accuracy score for later comparison.

Figure 41a—Blank keyboard quiz for PCs; 41b—for Chromebook

Handwriting vs. Keyboarding

_____By a show of hands, who thinks they type faster than they handwrite? By 8th grade, everyone should. If they handwrite faster, they probably don't like typing, and vice versa.

_____Today, students will compare these two by typing and writing a document. Why measure both?

_____Warm up with keyboarding. Review posture and hand position.

_____Open TypingTest.com or similar. Students take a three-minute quiz. Let them independently determine how to do this (if they haven't before). When done, they record their speeds on a common spreadsheet that's shared with you (like *Figure 42*):

Figure 42—Spreadsheet for Handwriting vs KB data

	A	B	C	D
1		Handwriting speed	Typing speed	Which is faster?
2	Masha	38	45	typing
3	Devon	40	65	typing
4	Sam	37	40	typing
5	Manda	36	34	handwriting
6				

_____Next: Students handwrite pages from a book being read in class to evaluate handwriting speed. Do this for three minutes (the same length as keyboarding). When done, students enter their speed into the same common shared spreadsheet.

_____Discuss purpose of this evaluation. How fast can anyone handwrite? The fastest 8th grader is probably around 35-40 wpm. How about typing speed? Many people type 45-100 wpm—or faster. What conclusion do students draw?

_____Post names of students who typed faster than they handwrote. Add to this list as students become proficient.

_____If students use workbooks, record speed/accuracy score for later comparison.

Keyboarding Challenge

_____Divide students into teams. Select a captain—this will be the only person who can answer questions. Responses must be quick—to show team knows the right key. See *Assessment* at end of this lesson.

_____Ask Team #1 a question, i.e.: *Which finger types f?* Give the team 3 seconds to answer (answer may be visual). If they can't, go to Team #2, but don't repeat question. If they don't know question or can't answer, move to Team #3 and then Team #4. If no one can answer, you can.

_____Next question goes to Team #2—even if they were the ones who answered Team #1's question. This is how teams get ahead. Pose question to Team #2 and repeat step above.

_____Sound dull? I thought so, but kids love it. Every time we play, it's a hit and they want more.

_____Prizes are optional.

Class exit ticket: **None.**

Differentiation

- *Assign a student to enter keyboarding assignment dates.*
- *Put Keyboard Challenge into a Jeopardy template.*
- *K-8 Keyboard Curriculum available in K-8 Keyboard Curriculum (available from Structured Learning).*

Assessment 9—Keyboarding quiz

KEYBOARDING SCOPE AND SEQUENCE CHECKLIST

Posture

____Copy to the side of keyboard; keyboard one inch off edge of table

____Correct posture—legs in front, body in front, elbows at sides, feet flat on floor

____Hands curled over home row, eyes on copy

Keyboarding

____Types 45 wpm by end of 8th grade, touch-typing all keys

____Types three pages in a single sitting at start of 8th grade

____Compose at keyboard with ease

____Demonstrate proper care and handling of keyboard

____Learn twenty basic keyboard shortcuts (Alt+F4, Esc, Ctrl+P, Ctrl+S, Ctrl+C, Ctrl+V, Ctrl+Alt+Del, Ctrl+B/I/U, double-click to enlarge window, Alt+Tab, Win key, Shift+tab, right mouse button key, Ctrl+ (zoom in), Ctrl- (zoom out), ???)

____Rest fingers on home row, reach for other keys. Hands appear still with fingers moving

____Understand all keyboard keys, arrow keys, and number pad

IMPORTANT KEYBOARD KEYS

Each bubble is worth two points. Fill in the bubble with one example of when you would use this key.

Your name _____

Your teacher _____

©AskaTechTeacher

Assessment 11—Blank keyboard quiz

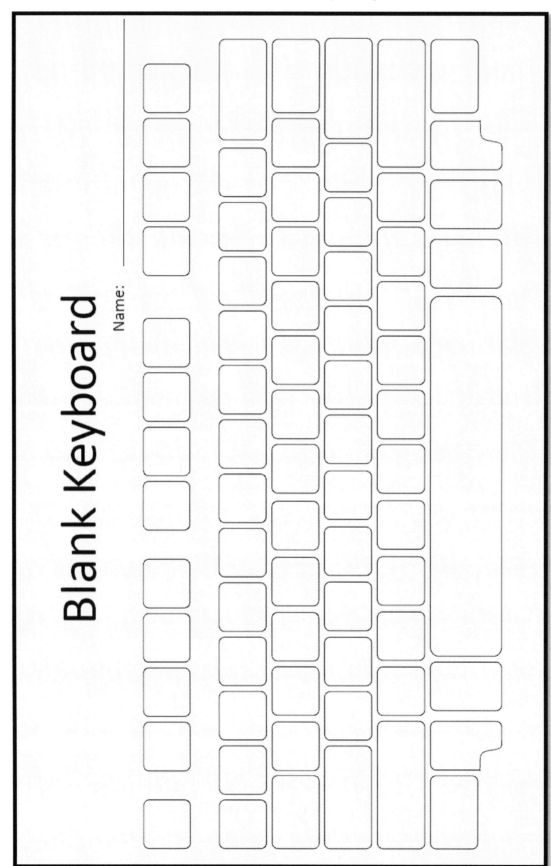

Blank Keyboard

Name:

Assessment 12—Chromebook blank keyboard quiz

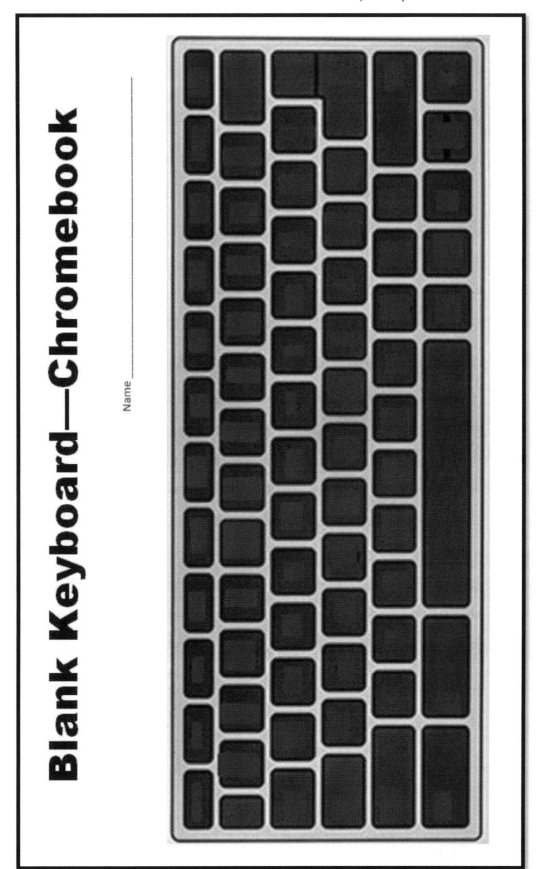

Blank Keyboard—Chromebook

Name

KEYBOARDING TEAM CHALLENGE

Review the following concepts. These are similar to questions that will be asked during the upcoming Team Challenge to find the year's most tech-savvy student!

1. What's the computer log in
2. What's computer password
3. What's password for TTL4
4. What row do your fingers start on
5. What row's above home row
6. What row's below home row
7. How do you find f and j without looking
8. Name 3 keys pinkie pushes
9. Name 3 keys ring finger pushes
10. Name 3 keys middle finger pushes
11. Name 3 keys pointer pushes
12. Name 1 key right thumb pushes
13. Which finger pushes backspace
14. Which finger pushes shift
15. Which finger pushes enter
16. Which finger pushes escape
17. 3 rules on how to sit at keyboard
18. Do you have cat's paws or dog paws at the computer
19. Why?
20. What part of the chair do you sit on when keyboarding
21. Where are your elbows when keyboarding
22. Where does right thumb rest
23. What is typing without looking at the keys called
24. Which finger pushes a
25. Which finger pushes b
26. Which finger pushes c
27. Which finger pushes d
28. Which finger pushes e
29. Which finger pushes f
30. Which finger pushes g
31. Which finger pushes h
32. Which finger pushes i
33. Which finger pushes j
34. Which finger pushes k
35. What finger pushes enter
36. What's the keyboard shortcut to exit
37. In general, which finger pushes a key
38. How do you capitalize
39. In general, do fingers or hands move to keys
40. Name a shortkey
41. What is a desktop

Article 14—5 Ways to make classroom keyboarding fun

5 Ways to Make Classroom Keyboarding Fun

The goal of typing isn't **speed and accuracy**. The goal is that students type well enough that it doesn't disrupt their thinking. Let me say that again:

The goal of keyboarding is students type well enough that it doesn't disrupt their thinking.

Much like breathing takes no thought and playing a piano is automatic, students want to be able to think while they type, fingers automatically moving to the keys that record their thoughts. Searching for key placement shouldn't interfere with how they develop a sentence. Sure, it does when students are just starting, but by third grade students should be comfortable enough with key placement to be working on speed.

To type as fast as the speed of thought isn't difficult. When referring to students in school, 'speed of thought' refers to how fast they develop ideas that will be recorded. 30 wpm is the low end. 45 wpm is good.

Students used to learn typing in high school, as a skill. Now, it's a tool for learning. So much of what we ask students to do on the way to authentic learning requires typing. Consider the academic need to:

- *write reports*
- *comment on Discussion Boards and blogs*
- *journal in blogs and online tools like Penzu*
- *research online (type addresses into a search bar)*
- *take digital notes (using Evernote, OneNote and similar)*
- *collaborate on Google Apps like Docs, Sheets, Presentations*
- *take online quizzes (like PARCC, SB)*

If you're a Common Core state, keyboarding shows up often in the Standards:

- *Starting in 4th grade, students must be able to type one page in a single sitting.*
- *By 3rd grade, keyboarding is used to **produce** work.'*
- *Keyboarding is required to take **Common Core Standards assessments** in the spring.*

The myth is that students will teach themselves when they need it. That's half right. They will teach themselves, but it won't necessarily be in time for their needs. If you're in a tech-infused school, it's your obligation to teach them the right way to type so they can organically develop the tools to support learning.

Most teachers roll out typing with a graduated program. In September of the new school year, students start Lesson 1. Sometime around May, they are through all the lessons and considered trained. Everything is on auto-pilot with little intervention from the teacher. That works for about ten percent of students. Those are the ones who are intrinsically motivated to learn and nothing gets in their way.

The other 90% need a little more help. Here are six ideas to make your typing lessons fun and effective:

Drill

Drill is part of every granular typing program. Students must learn key placement, finger usage, posture, and all those other details.

There are a lot of options for this—both free like Typing Web and fee-based like QwertyTown. Students usually start enthusiastically, which wanes within a few months as it becomes more of the same rote practice.

Games

When your organic typing program shows signs of wearing on students, throw in a sprinkling of games that teach key placement, speed and accuracy. Big Brown Bear is great for youngers; NitroTyping for olders, and Popcorn Typer for the in-between grades of 2nd-5th.

Offer games sporadically, not on a schedule. Make it a reward for keyboarding benchmarks.

Team Challenge

Students work in teams to answer keyboard-related questions in a game show format. You can use a Jeopardy template that includes not only keyboard questions, but shortkeys that students use often.

Integrate into Class Inquiry

Within a month of starting a keyboarding program, have students use their growing skills authentically in class projects. This can be book reports, research, a brochure for history class, or a collaborative document through Google Apps. The keyboarding is a tool to communicate knowledge in a subject, much like a pencil, an artist brush or a violin. The better their keyboarding skills, the easier it is to complete the meat of the project, like a blog response, trading cards on characters in a book, or a family tree.

Remind students to use their keyboarding skills to make this real-life experience easier—hands on their own side of the keyboard, use all fingers, good posture, elbows at their sides. Let their team of grade level teachers know what traits to look for as students research in class or the library. Get parents to reinforce it at home.

ASCII Art

ASCII Art uses keyboarding skills to create artistic representations of class learning. This is a fun way to use keyboarding in other classes. All students do is find a picture that represents the class inquiry topic being addressed, put it as a watermark into the word processing program, type over the washed out image with a variety of keys, then delete the watermark. This takes about thirty minutes usually and always excites students with the uniqueness of their work.

How to Prepare Students for Year-end Tests

As part of my online tech teacher persona, I get lots of questions from readers about how to make technology work in an educational environment. This one from Terry is probably on the minds of thousands of teachers:

> *Any help for identifying and re-enforcing tech skills needed to take the online PARCC tests (coming in 2014-15)? Even a list of computer terms would help; copy, cut, paste, highlight, select; use of keys like tab, delete, insert; alt, ctrl and shift. There does not seem to be any guidelines as to prepping students on the "how to's" of taking an online test and reading and understanding the directions. It would be great to take advantage of the time we have before the PARCC's become a reality. Thanks!*

Every spring, more than 4 million students in 36 states and the District of Columbia will take near-final versions of the PARCC and Smarter Balanced efforts to test Common Core State Standards learning in the areas of mathematics and English/language arts. Tests will be administered via digital devices (though there are options for paper-and-pencil). The tests won't produce detailed scores of student performance (that starts next year), but this field-testing is crucial to finding out what works and doesn't in this comprehensive assessment tool, including the human factors like techphobia and sweaty palms (from both students and teachers).

After I got Terry's email, I polled my PLN to find specific tech areas students needed help with in preparing for the Assessments. It boils down to five tech areas:

Keyboarding

Students need to have enough familiarity with the keyboard that they know where keys are, where the number pad is, where the F row is, how keys are laid out. They don't need to be touch typists or even facilely use all fingers. Just have them comfortable enough they have a good understanding of where all the pieces are. Starting next school year, have them type fifteen minutes a week in a class setting and 45 minutes a week using keyboarding for class activities (homework, projects—that sort). That'll do it.

Basic computer skills

These skills—drag-and-drop, keyboarding with speed and accuracy, highlighting, playing videos—are not easy for a student if they haven't had an instructive course in using computers. It won't surprise any adult when I say using and iPad isn't the same as using a computer. The former has a bunch more buttons and tools and the latter more intuitive. And typing on an iPad virtual keyboard is not the same as the reassuring clackity-clack of a traditional set-up. Will students get used to that? Yes, but not this month.

Make sure students are technologically proficient in their use of a variety of digital devices, including computers, Chromebooks, and iPads. This means students have an understanding of what defines a digital device, how it operates, what type of programs are used on various types (for example, apps are for iPads and software for computers) and how do they operate, and what's the best way to scaffold them for learning? Being comfortable with technology takes time and practice. Make digital devices and tech solutions available at every opportunity—for note-taking, backchannel communications, quick assessments, online collaboration, even timing an activity. Make it part of a student's educational landscape.

One area Terry asks about is vocabulary. The words she mentioned—*copy, paste, cut, highlight*—these are domain-specific. Use the correct terminology as you teach but observe students. If they don't understand what you're saying, help them decode it with context, affixes, or an online dictionary for geek words. Keep a list of those words. Soon, you'll have a vocabulary list for technology that's authentic and specific to your needs.

Stamina

Expect students to type for extended periods without complaint. Common Core requires this. That's what 'one page in a sitting in 4th grade, 2 pages in a sitting in 5th grade, 3 pages in a sitting in 6th grade' means. The Assessments expect students have that sort of stamina. They're long tests with lots of keyboarding and other tech skills. Make sure your students have practiced working at computers for extended periods.

A good idea is to have students take some online assessments prior to this summative one. These can be created by the teacher using any number of online tools like Google Forms or use already-created tests like those that follow BrainPop videos.

Problem Solving

Make sure students know what to do when a tech problem arises. They should be able to handle simple problems like 'headphones don't work' or 'caps lock won't turn on' or 'my document froze'. This is easily accomplished by having students take responsibility for solving tech problems, with the teacher acting as a resource. They will soon be able to differentiate between what they have the ability to handle and what requires assistance.

A great starting point when teaching problem solving is the Common Core Standards for Mathematical Practice. These are aligned with the Math Standards but apply to all facets of learning.

Teacher Training

Make sure teachers administering the online tests are familiar with them and comfortable in that world. They should know how to solve basic tech issues that arise without calling for outside help. This is effectively accomplished by having teachers use technology in their classroom on a regular basis for class activities, as a useful tool in their educational goals. Helps teachers make this happen.

Lesson #4-5 Problem Solving

Vocabulary	Problem solving	Homework
• Authentic problems • Conjecture • Deductive reasoning • Democratic society • Inductive reasoning • Mathematical language • Proportional reasoning • Responsible citizen • Visual learner	• What's the difference between 'save' and 'save-as'? • Why 'save early save often'? • Which tool do I use (what works best?) • It's confusing (ask a friend to explain why they like it) • I couldn't get on the keyboarding website (try another one) • I tried to solve the problem (try another strategy; failure is fine)	Review word processing, quotes, problem-solving strategies (for quiz) Select problem/date for Problem-solving Board Review webtools and know which you will use Keyboard for 45 minutes, 15 minutes at a time
Academic Applications Critical thinking, math, other academic topics	**Required Skills** Familiarity with speaking and listening standards, problem solving, online tools, digital citizenship	**Standards** CCSS: Stds for Math.Practice NETS: 4a, 5c

Essential Question

How does tech teach problem solving and logical thinking?

Big Idea

Make things as simple as possible, but not simpler (Albert Einstein)

Teacher Preparation/Materials Required

- Have backchannel available.
- Have Problem-solving Board rubrics, online sign-up.
- Have lesson materials online to preview.
- Update class calendar with activities.
- Integrate domain-specific tech vocabulary into lesson.
- Ensure all required links are on student digital devices.
- Ask what tech problems students had difficulty with.
- Something happen you weren't prepared for? Show how you react with a positive attitude.
- Know which tasks weren't completed last week and whether they are necessary to move forward.

Assessment Strategies

- Previewed required material; came to class prepared
- Annotated workbook (if using)
- Signed up for Board
- Worked well in a group
- Completed warm-up, exit ticket
- Joined classroom conversations
- [tried to] solve own problems
- Decisions followed class rules
- Left room as s/he found it
- Higher order thinking: analysis, evaluation, synthesis
- Habits of mind observed

Steps

Time required: *90-270 minutes, spread throughout the class grading period*
Class warm-up: *Keyboard on class typing program, paying attention to posture*

This lesson is part of many lessons—not a stand-alone.

_____Homework is assigned before class so students are prepared for class projects.

_____Use a backchannel program like Socrative_to determine student understanding

_____Review articles at the end of this lesson, *How to Teach Students to Problem Solve, 5 Must-have Skills for New Teachers,* and *Let Students Learn From Failure.*

_____Any homework questions? Have students sign up for Problem-solving presentation via class Google Calendar (if you don't have Google Apps, use Sign-up Genius or similar).

_____Call on students to share how to solve problems—oral quick quiz.

_____Discuss what it means to be a 'problem solver'. Who do students go to when they need a problem solved? Do students believe that person gets it right more often than others? Would they believe most people are wrong half the time?

_____Problem solving is closely aligned with logical thinking, critical thinking, reasoning, and thought habits. Discuss why students should become problem solvers (hint: refer to prior point—most people students go to for assistance are wrong half the time). Discuss characteristics of a 'problem solver' (from Common Core):

- *attend to precision*
- *value evidence*
- *comprehend and critique*
- *demonstrate independence*

- *make sense of problems and persevere in solving them*
- *use appropriate tools strategically*
- *understand other perspectives*

_____Discuss 'Big Idea'—quote from Albert Einstein. Discuss great quotes about problem solving in *Figure 43 (full size at the end of the lesson).*

Figure 43—Problem-solving quotes

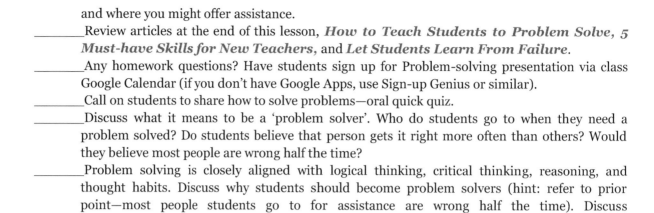

_____Discuss shortkeys (from *Keyboarding* lesson). How are they problem solving? Demonstrate this by asking students to tell you how to perform a skill. Is it easier to share the shortkey?

_____Discuss problem-solving strategies:

- o *Act out a problem*
- o *Break a problem into parts*
- o *Draw a diagram*
- o *Guess and check*
- o *Observe and collect data*
- o *See patterns*
- o *Think logically*

- o *Try to solve before asking for help*
- o *Try, fail, try again*
- o *Use Help files*
- o *Use tools available*
- o *Distinguish relevant from irrelevant information*
- o *Use what has worked in past*
- o *Work backwards*

_____See *Figure 44* for '***How to Solve a Problem***' (full size in appendix):

Figure 44—How to solve a problem

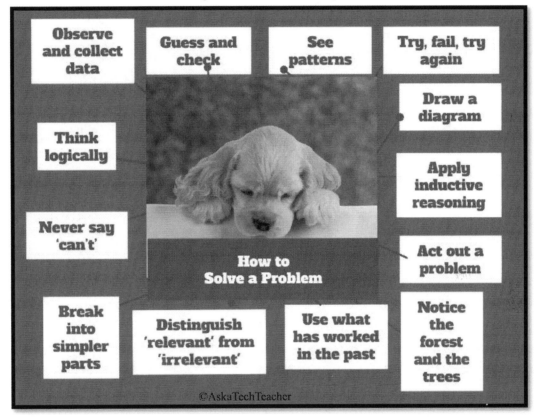

_____When students face a problem, use *Figure 44* strategies to solve it before asking for assistance.

_____Here are two projects to reinforce problem solving in everyday life:

- • *Problem-solving board*
- • *Analysis of authentic problem-solving skills*

Problem-solving Board

_____Students teach classmates common problems faced when using technology. Ideally, you have collected these throughout the year from students, other teachers, and parents—the types of problems that stopped students as they tried to use tech in their education journey. This list might include (*Figure 45*):

Figure 45—Common tech problems

Problem	
My browser is too small	I can't find a tool
Browser toolbar missing	My screen is frozen
Can't exit a program	My menu command is grey
What's today's date	Can't find Bold, Italic
Double click doesn't work	Can't find the program
Start button disappeared	Internet toolbar's gone
Program disappeared	My computer doesn't work
Erased my document	My programs are gone

_____See a longer list at end of lesson. By the end of 8th grade, students should know all of these.

_____Students, working in groups, select a problem from the list you provide that they will teach classmates, and then select the date they'll do it. You can provide sign-up forms via a Padlet wall embedded into the class start page (*Figure 46a*), SignUp Genius, a shared spreadsheet (*Figure 46b),* or another method that works for you.

Figure 46a-b—Problem-solving Board sign-ups

_____***Note: Throughout the year, keep a list of problems for next year's Board.***

_____Student groups use one of the online tools they are familiar with from earlier grades or prior lessons in eighth grade in their presentation. This may include:

Figure 47a—Prezi presentation; 47b—Photocube; 47c—Screenshot

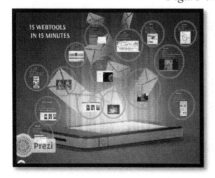

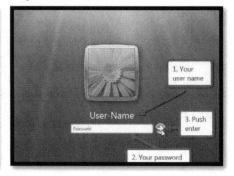

- *Animoto or a video*
- *Comics*
- *online slideshow*
- *Photocube (Figure 47b)*

- *Prezi (Figure 47a)*
- *Scratch*
- *a screencast or screenshot (Figure 47c)*
- *SketchUp*

_____Students can get solutions from family, friends, or online sources.

_____Students pay attention to these considerations when preparing project:

- *Determine target audience, goal, and purpose of presentation.*
- *Download and use public domain clipart.*
- *Work as a team.*

_____Each project is expected to:

- *convey information, offer insights and analysis*
- *organize content so that problem solution is evident*
- *use headings, illustrations, and multimedia, as well as text to teach*
- *introduce presentation with one or several of the problem-solving quotes*

Figure 48—Problem-solving Board rubric

PROBLEM SOLVING BOARD
Grading Rubric

Name: _____

Knew question	_____
Use problem solving strategies to solve problem	_____
Sequenced ideas logically in arriving at solution	_____
Looked audience in eye	_____
No umm's, stutters	_____
No nervous movements (giggles, wiggles, etc.)	_____
Demonstrated command of language	_____
Answered audience questions with evidence	_____
Overall	_____

_____During presentation, students will:

- *Present in a focused manner with descriptions, facts, details, and examples.*
- *Use appropriate eye contact, adequate volume, and clear pronunciation.*
- *Adapt speech to the context and task.*
- *Take questions. The audience is responsible for making sure speaker makes sense.*

_____Student groups get three class periods to organize, produce and share project via embed into blog or website. Use a fourth class for presentations.

_____Entire presentation takes about three minutes. *Figure 48 (Assessment* at the end of this lesson*)* is a sample of the rubric you can fill out from your iPad.

_____Review digital rights and responsibilities before using the internet search functions. Include citations to any media shared with students.

Analysis of authentic problem-solving skills

_____During the grading period, student identify five-ten problems faced in any part of their life—home, school, or personal—and what problem-solving strategy they used to solve it. They'll record them in a spreadsheet shared with classmates and the teacher. Data curated with include (see *Assessment 14a-b* for examples):

- *what tech problem they faced*
- *how they solved it*
- *what strategy they used from the list*
- *any additional comments*

_____At the end of class, it will be a resource students can draw on for future problems.

_____Here's how this works:

- *Student records 5-10 problems faced during the grading period in a Google Spreadsheet created by you and shared with students.*
- *Student answers a Google Forms poll (like* Assessment 14a) *that you share.*
- *They must have 5-10 of these during the grading period.*

Assessment 14a-b—Problem solving authentic data

_____Throughout class, check for understanding.

Class exit ticket: *Enter one problem into Google Form.*

Differentiation

- *Have one student create Google Form for Problem Solving to be used to track class results.*
- *Add 'other' to the poll and let students share their own unique strategy with classmates.*
- *If student can't attend class (say, parent's car doesn't start), they can present via a virtual classroom like Google Hangout.*
- *Student has a problem they'd like to share that isn't from the list. If it relates to the education journey, consider allowing it (maybe they'd like to share how to run a Google Hangout).*

Assessment 15—Problem-solving Board

PROBLEM-SOLVING BOARD
Rubric

Name: _____

Problem solved: _____

Knew question   _____

Knew answer   _____

Asked audience for help if didn't know answer   _____

No umm's, stutters   _____

No nervous movements (giggles, wiggles, etc.)   _____

No slang   _____

Overall   _____

Figure 49—Common tech problems

Common problems students face with computers

	Problem	Solution
1.	My browser is too small	Double click blue bar
2.	Browser toolbar missing	Push F11
3.	Can't exit a program	Alt+F4
4.	What's today's date	Hover over clock Shift+Alt+D in Word
5.	Double click doesn't work	Push enter
7.	Start button disappeared	Use Windows button
8.	Program disappeared	Check taskbar
9.	Erased my document	Ctrl+Z
10.	I can't find a tool	Right click on screen; it'll show most common tools
11.	My screen is frozen	Clear a dialogue box Press Escape four times
12.	My menu command is grey	Press escape 4 times and try again
13.	Can't find Bold, Italic, Underline	Use Ctrl+B, Ctrl+I, Ctrl+U
14.	Can't find the program	Push Start, use 'Search' field
15.	Internet toolbar's gone	Push F11
16.	My computer doesn't work	Check monitor/tower power, plugs
17.	My programs are gone	Are you logged in correctly?

Assessment 16—Problem-solving presentation rubric

Problem-solving Presentation Assessment

Problem solving: Webtool used: Strategy used:		Student/Team:			

Pts	Investigate	Design	Plan	Create	Evaluate	Group
0	Team does not complete investigation to standard discussed in class	Team does not complete design to standard discussed in class	Team does not complete plan to standard discussed in class	Team does not complete work to standard discussed in class	Team does not complete evaluation to standard discussed in class	Team does not work together to standard discussed in class
1-2	Team states problem but not clearly, vaguely, understanding skills required. Students have difficulty verbalizing steps required to complete	Team addresses some detail about how project will be presented with selected tool, but leaves critical elements out	Team project plan contains some goals for completing project; timeline is not sustainable	Team creates at least part of storyboard, timeline, product/solution	Team evaluates product/solution as they work, but does not adapt plan or project to problems that arise	Team occasionally works well as a group, but has difficulty allocating work and arriving at consensus
3-4	Team states problem clearly with a strong understanding of skills required. Team shows evidence of researching and describes solution in detail	Team addresses all specifics required to create a how-to and present to class	Team produces a plan that contains a clear and achievable goal for using time wisely during class	Team uses appropriate techniques and equipment, storyboard is effective. Team follows plan, and modifies when required, resulting in good quality project	Team evaluates how-to project and their performance; suggests ways to improve, and tests solution before presenting to class	Team frequently incorporates group member input into project, showing respect for the value of all members
Total						**/20**

Figure 50—Great quotes about problem solving

Great Quotes About Problem Solving

Success consists of going from failure to failure without loss of enthusiasm.

— Winston Churchill

In times like these it is good to remember that there have always been times like these.

— Paul Harvey *Broadcaster*

Never try to solve all the problems at once — make them line up for you one-by-one.

— Richard Sloma

Some problems are so complex that you have to be highly intelligent and well-informed just to be undecided about them.

— Laurence J. Peter

Life is a crisis - so what!

— Malcolm Bradbury

You don't drown by falling in the water; you drown by staying there.

— Edwin Louis Cole

The significant problems we face cannot be solved at the same level of thinking we were at when we created them.

— Albert Einstein

It is not stress that kills us. It is effective adaptation to stress that allows us to live.

— George Vaillant

The most serious mistakes are not being made as a result of wrong answers. The truly dangerous thing is asking the wrong questions.

— Peter Drucker *Men, Ideas & Politics*

Eighty percent of success is showing up.

—Woody Allen

The problem is not that there are problems. The problem is expecting otherwise and thinking that having problems is a problem.

—Theodore Rubin

On the infrequent occasions when I have been called upon … to play the bongo drums, the introducer never seems to find it necessary to mention that I also do theoretical physics.

—Richard Feynman

Do not keep saying to yourself, if you can possibly avoid it, "But how can it be like that?" because you will get "down the drain," into a blind alley from which nobody has yet escaped. Nobody knows how it can be like that.

—Richard Feynman

The problem is not that there are problems. The problem is expecting otherwise and thinking that having problems is a problem.

— Theodore Rubin

It's not that I'm so smart; it's just that I stay with problems longer.

—Albert Einstein

There is a great difference between worry and concern. A worried person sees a problem, and a concerned person solves a problem.

—Harold Stephens

While average people are thinking negatively about problems, successful people view their problems positively. They love problems. They eat them for breakfast.

Why? Because problems create value; the more problems you can solve, the more valuable you will be, the more money you will make, the more responsibility you will have.

—Brian Klemmer

No problem can stand the assault of sustained thinking.

—Voltaire

Problems are only opportunities with thorns on them.

—Hugh Miller

Article 16—How to Teach Students to Solve Problems

How to Teach Students to Solve Problems

Of all the skills students learn in school, **problem solving** arguably is the most valuable and the hardest to learn. It's fraught with uncertainty—what if the student looks stupid as he tries? What if everyone's watching and he can't do it—isn't it better not to try? What if it works, but not the way Everyone wants it to? When you're a student, it's understandable when they decide to let someone tell them what to do.

But this isn't the type of learner we want to build. We want risk-takers, those willing to be the load-bearing pillar of the class. And truthfully, by a certain age, kids want to make up their own mind. Our job as teachers is to provide the skills necessary for them to make wise, effective decisions.

It's not a stand-alone subject. It starts with a habit of inquiry in all classes—math, LA, history, science, any of them. I constantly ask students questions, get them to think and evaluate, provide evidence that supports process as well as product. Whether they're writing, reading, or creating an art project, I want them thinking what they're doing and why.

Common Core puts problem solving front and center. It comes up in ELA ("*Students will be challenged and asked questions that push them to refer back to what they've read. This stresses critical-thinking, problem-solving, and analytical skills that are required for success in college, career, and life.*"), but is inescapable in Math. In fact, students cannot fully meet the Math Standards without understanding how to effectively approach the unknown. Consider the Standards for Mathematical Practice that overlay all grade levels K-12:

- *Make sense of problems and persevere in solving them*
- *Reason abstractly and quantitatively*
- *Construct viable arguments and critique the reasoning of others*
- *Model*
- *Use appropriate tools strategically*
- *Attend to precision*
- *Look for and make use of structure*
- *Look for and express regularity in repeated reasoning*

Do these sound like great strategies for more than math? How about deciding what classes to take? Or whether to make a soccer or basketball game on the weekend? Or which college to attend? Using these eight tools strategically, with precision, and tenaciously is a great first step.

The question becomes: How do students **learn to use them**? Certainly, as they accomplish their grade-level math curriculum, you as teacher remind them they aren't doing a multiplication problem (or an Algebra one); rather they're reasoning abstractly or using appropriate tools strategically or expressing regularity in repeated reasoning. But for deep learning, hands-on authentic experience is required. Let's say, for example, the class is investigating the purchase of an MP3 player. Should they purchase an iPad, a smartphone, a dedicated use MP3 player, or a different option? How do students arrive at a decision—solve that problem? Ask students to work through the steps below as they address a decision. Ask them to note where they accomplish one or more of the Standards for Mathematical Practice above:

1. What do you want in an MP3 player? Should it play music, show videos, pictures, communicate with others, be a phone also? Make that list so you know how to evaluate information as you collect it (**compare/contrast**).

2. What do you know about the topic (**evidence**)? Have you seen some you liked or didn't like? What have you heard about those on your list? You are a good resource to yourself. Don't discount that. You'll be surprised how much you know on a variety of topics. This step is important to college and career. Future employers and schools want you to think, to use your intelligence and your knowledge to evaluate and solve problems.

3. What advice do knowledgeable friends have (**perspective taking, collaboration**)? You want the input of MP3 users. Your friends will think whatever they own is the best, because they're vested in that choice, but listen to their evidence and the conclusions they draw based on that. This is important to a team-oriented environment. Listen to all sides, even if you don't agree.

4. **Dig deeper (close reading)**. Check other resources (**uncover knowledge**). This includes:
   o *people who don't like the product*
   o *online sources. Yep, you might as well get used to online research if you aren't yet. Statistics show more people get their news from blogs than traditional media (newspapers, TV) and you know where blogs are.*
   o *your parents who will bring up topics friends didn't, like cost, longevity, reliability*

5. **Evaluate your resources (integration of knowledge)**. How much money do you have? Eliminate the choices that don't fit your constraints (money, time, use, etc.) If there are several choices that seem to work, this will help you make the decision. You might have to save money or get a job so you can afford the one you've chosen. Or you might decide to settle for a cheaper version. Just make sure you are aware of how you made the choice and are satisfied with it.

6. What are the **risks involved** in making the decision (**reflection**)? Maybe buying an MP3 player means you can't do something else you wanted. Are you comfortable with that choice?

7. **Make a decision (transfer learning)**. That's right. Make a decision and live with it knowing you've considered all available information and evaluated it logically and objectively.

Optionally, you might have students evaluate problem solving in their favorite game, say, Minecraft. All it requires is that as they play, think about what they're doing:

- *What is the goal of Minecraft? How is it best achieved*
- *What does the student know about playing the game that can be used in achieving the goal?*
- *Does working with friends and gaining feedback make life easier in Minecraft?*
- *How does experience in the game affect progress?*
- *And so on...*

This is how students become the problem solvers required of their Future. When the day comes that how they solve a problem affects the direction their life takes (college, career, marriage, children, a tattoo), they'll be happy to have strategies that make it easier.

Article 17—5 Must-have Skills for New Tech Teachers

5 Must-have Skills for New Tech Teachers

If you teach technology, it's likely you were thrown into it by your Admin. You used to be a first grade teacher or the science expert or maybe even the librarian and suddenly, you walked into school one day and found out you'd become that tech person down the hall you were always in awe of, the one responsible for classroom computers, programs, curriculum, and everything in between. Now that's you—the go-to person for tech problems, computer quirks, crashes and freezes, and tech tie-ins for classroom inquiry.

You have no idea where to begin.

Here's a peek into your future: On that first propitious day, everything will change. Your colleagues will assume you received a data upload of the answers to every techie question. It doesn't matter that yesterday, you were one of them. Now, you will be on a pedestal, colleague's necks craned upward as they ask: *How do I get the class screen to work? We need microphones for a lesson I'm starting in three minutes. Can you please-please-please fix them?* You will nod your head, smile woodenly, and race to your classroom for the digital manuals (if you're lucky) or Google for online help.

Let me start by saying: Don't worry. Really. You'll learn by doing, just as we teach students. Take a deep breath, engage your brain, and let your brilliance shine.

That's the number one skill—confidence—but there are five other practical strategies that have worked for those who came before you. Consider:

Be a communicator

Talk to grade-level teachers weekly. Scaffold your lessons with what they teach. Ask them to stay during tech class and offer on-the-spot tie-ins between what you teach and they say in class. Yes, they might want/need the time for planning or meetings, but the benefit to students of this team-teaching approach is tremendous. And it benefits the teachers, also. Many of them are not yet sold on integrating tech into their classrooms. They know they must if they're in one of the 46 Common Core adoptive states, but they don't like it, don't know how to do it, and don't see why it's so important. When they see you do it, they will be more willing to weave it into their lessons. For example, when they hear how you reinforce good keyboarding skills, they will be more likely to insist on those traits in their classroom.

Be a risk-taker

Flaunt your cheeky geekiness. Start a Twitter feed. Use your iPhone as a timer or the iPad to scan in an art project for a digital portfolio. At any opportunity, share your geek glee. Let them see that tech is part of life, not a subject taught in school. It's a habit, a time-saver, a facilitator, a joy. It won't take long to convert them. A couple of admiring glances from friends or appreciative thanks from parents and they'll be sold.

Be an explorer

Go to the grade-level classrooms and demonstrate how technology is part of learning. This can be via iPads, the class pod of computers, the netbooks, or whatever is available. Ask students what they are doing in class and offer tech methods to make it easier. For example, are they submitting homework in a pile on the teacher's desk? Try a drop box—or email. Could they type reports instead of handwrite them (I know—this gets philosophic, so be prepared for that discussion)? Instead of hand-drawn posters where success leans toward the artistically-talented, could they use Glogster? Encourage students to plug in during class.

Be a negotiator

You need parental buy-in on tech ed, but it is a topic typically outside their comfort zone. I often hear from 2nd grade parents that their children know more than they do (I'm talking MS Office, internet use, and some online tools). Understand that this frightens them and part of your job is to mitigate their fears. Here are some ideas:

- Have your door always open. Be ready and willing to talk with them about how to complete their child's projects—not so they can do for them, but so they feel it is within their child's grasp. Take as long as needed and welcome them to return.
- Answer parent tech questions, even if it's about a home computer. My experience is these are often simple but intimidating. If you mitigate fear, you maximize support for tech ed.
- Offer a parent class to teach skills students are learning. Listen to your group. What makes these intelligent adults nervous about tech? Solve it for them. I often start with an agenda and end with a free-for-all, where I answer questions or help parents create fliers for soccer teams or solve home-based tech problems. It's all good. They leave feeling I'm a partner.

Don't take life too seriously

Have a sense of humor about everything. You're going to have computer meltdowns. It's why robots can't replace teachers, so embrace chaos. One of the true joys of tech is the puzzling. Why doesn't the mouse work? Why does a website work on one computer and not another? Where'd the taskbar go? Let students see how much fun it is to engage the brain.

Article 18—Let Students Learn From Failure
Let Students Learn From Failure

Too often, students—and teachers—believe learning comes from success when in truth, it's as likely to be the product of failure. Knowing what doesn't work is a powerful weapon as we struggle to think critically about the myriad issues along our path to college and/or career. As teachers, it's important we reinforce the concept that learning has many faces. Here are ten ways to teach through failure:

Use the Mulligan Rule

What's the Mulligan Rule? Any golfers? A mulligan in golf is a do-over. Blend that concept into your classroom. Common Core expects students to write-edit-resubmit. Make that part of every lesson. After submittal, give students a set amount of time to redo and resubmit their work. Some won't, but those who do will learn much more by the process.

Don't define success as perfection

When you're discussing a project or a lesson, don't define it in terms of checkboxes or line items or 100% accuracy. Think about your favorite book. Is it the same as your best friend's? How about the vacation you're planning—would your sister pick that dream location? Education is no different. Many celebrated 'successful' people failed at school because they were unusual thinkers. Most famously: Bill Gates, who dropped out of college because he believed he could learn more from life than professors.

Education pedagogists categorize these sorts of ideas as ***higher-order thinking*** and ***Habits of Mind***—traits that contribute to critical thinking, problem solving, and thriving. These are difficult to quantify on a report card, but critical to life-long success. Observe students as they work. Notice their risk-taking curiosity, how they color outside the lines. Anecdotally assess their daily efforts and let that count as much as a summative exam that judges a point in time.

Let students see you fail

One reason lots of teachers keep the same lesson plans year-to-year is they are vetted. The teacher won't be surprised by a failure or a question they can't answer. Honestly, this is a big reason why many eschew technology: Too often, it fails at just that critical moment.

Revise your mindset. Don't hide your failures from students. Don't apologize. Don't be embarrassed or defeated. Show them how you recover from failure. Model the steps you take to move to Plan B, C, even X. Show your teaching grit and students will understand that, too, is what they're learning: How to recover from failure.

Share strategies for problem solving

Problems are inevitable. Everyone has them. What many people DON'T have is a strategy to address them. Share these with students. Post these on the classroom wall. When students have problems, suggest they try a strategy from this list, and then another, and another. Eventually, the problem will resolve, the result of a tenacious, gritty attack by an individual who refuses to give up.

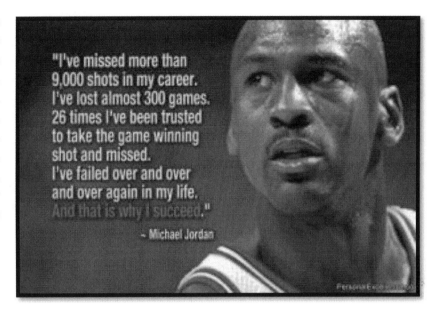

"I've missed more than 9,000 shots in my career. I've lost almost 300 games. 26 times I've been trusted to take the game winning shot and missed. I've failed over and over and over again in my life. And that is why I succeed."

– Michael Jordan

Exult in problems

If you're geeky, you love problems, puzzles, and the maze that leads from question to answer. It doesn't intimidate or frighten you, it energizes you. Share that enthusiasm with students. They are as likely to meet failure as success in their lives; show them your authentic, granular approach to addressing that eventuality.

Assess grit

Success isn't about right and wrong. More often, it's about grit—tenacity, working through a process, and not giving up when failure seems imminent. Statistically, over half of people say they 'succeeded' (in whatever venture they tried) not by being the best in the field but because they were the last man standing.

Integrate that into your lessons. Assess student effort, their attention to detail, their ability to transfer knowledge from earlier lessons to this one, their enthusiasm for learning, how often they tried-failed-retried, and that they completed the project. Let students know they will be evaluated on those criteria more than the perfection of their work.

Let students teach each other

There are many paths to success. Often, what works for one person is based on their perspective, personal history, and goals. This is at the core of differentiation: that we communicate in multiple ways—visually, orally, tactilely—in an effort to reach all learning styles.

Even so, students may not understand. Our failure to speak in a language they understand will become their failure to learn the material. Don't let that happen. Let students be the teachers. They often pick a relationship or comparison you wouldn't think of. Let students know that in your classroom, brainstorming and freedom of speech are problem-solving strategies.

Don't be afraid to move the goal posts

Even if it's in the middle of a lesson. That happens all the time in life and no one apologizes, feels guilty, or accommodates your anger. When you teach a lesson, you constantly reassess based on student progress. Do the same with assessment.

But make it fair. Let students know the changes are rooted in your desire that they succeed. If you can't make that argument, you probably shouldn't make the change.

Success is as much serendipity as planning

Think of Velcro and post-it notes—life-changing products resulting from errors. They surprised their creators and excited the world. Keep those possibilities available to students.

Don't reward speed

Often, students who finish first are assigned the task of helping neighbors or playing time-filler games. Finishing early should not be rewarded. Or punished. Sometimes it means the student thoroughly understood the material. Sometimes it means they glossed over it. Students are too often taught finishing early is a badge of honor, a mark of their expertise. Remove that judgment and let it be what it is.

Lesson #6-8 Digital Citizenship

Vocabulary	Problem solving	Homework
• Benchmark • Cloud • Cracker/hacker • Creative Commons • Cyberbullying • Digital citizen • Digital footprint • Digital native • IP address • Keywords • Netiquette • Plagiarism • Social media	• How do I share a project ('embed') • Keywords don't work (think deeper about topic) • Why be a good digital citizen if no one knows who I am (note to self: do right thing even when no one's looking) • Everyone shares pictures (until they learn their lesson) • We were just having fun (does cyberbully victim agree?) • Parent won't allow n social media • If I can't find citation, can I use text/image? (It depends)	Create a Tagxedo with digcit words Review notes to prepare for project Watch all videos; prepare reflections Keyboard 45 minutes, 15 minutes at a time Review copyright law

Academic Applications	Required Skills	Standards
research, collaboration, sharing, online safety	Familiarity with social media, internet, keyboarding, digital citizenship	CCSS: WHST.6-8.8 NETS: 2a-d

Essential Question

What are the rights and responsibilities of a Digital Citizen?

Big Idea

Just as in the physical world, the digital world bestows rights and requires responsibilities

Teacher Preparation/Materials Required

- Have links to all digcit resources on class start page.
- Integrate domain-specific tech vocabulary into lesson.
- Have lesson materials online to preview.
- Know whether you need extra time to complete lesson.
- Have student workbooks available (if using).
- Ask what tech problems students had difficulty with.
- Talk with grade-level team to tie into internet inquiry.
- Know which tasks weren't completed last week and whether they are necessary to move forward.
- Something happen you weren't prepared for? Show students how you fix the emergency without a meltdown and with a positive attitude.

Assessment Strategies

- Previewed required material; came to class prepared
- Completed blog posts and commented on classmates
- Completed digcit projects
- Created original artwork with an online graphics program
- Worked independently
- Used good keyboarding habits
- Completed warm-up, exit ticket
- Joined classroom conversations
- Higher order thinking: analysis, evaluation, synthesis
- Habits of mind observed

Steps

Time required: *270 minutes or more, spread throughout the year*
Class warm-up: *Keyboarding on the class typing program*

This lesson can be sprinkled throughout the year rather than taught as a unit.

_____**Homework is assigned the week before this unit so students are prepared.**

_____Any questions from homework? Expect students to review unit and come to class ready.

_____Use backchannel program like Socrative to determine student understanding and where you might offer assistance.

Figure 3--Tagxedo

_____Expect this discussion to take most of two classes; leave two weeks (four classes) for the projects.

_____Discuss Tagxedo homework created with DigCit words (*Figure 51*).

_____Give students three minutes to Tweet their thoughts about any of the DigCit topics (if you have a class Twitter account).

_____Goals for this unit include:

- *Students understand human, cultural, and societal issues related to technology and practice legal/ethical behavior.*
- *Students exhibit a positive attitude toward technology, a mindset that supports collaboration, learning and productivity.*
- *Students advocate and practice safe, legal, and responsible use of information.*
- *Students understand 'digital footprint'.*
- *Students demonstrate personal responsibility for lifelong learning.*
- *Students understand part they play in preventing cyberbullying.*
- *Students use internet legally to gather information.*
- *Students use technology and digital media strategically and capably.*

_____Discuss what it means to be a good digital citizen. Why is this important if no one knows who you are? Must you be honest if you're anonymous? Who does it hurt? What does *Figure 52* mean—a quote by legendary football coach, John Wooden?

Figure 52—Personal responsibility quote

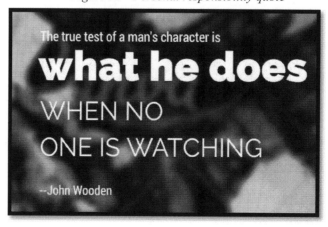

_____Throughout the school year when relevant, discuss the topics listed in *Figure 53* under '8th grade'. If you haven't covered K-7 topics, discuss those before moving into 8th grade material.

They scaffold learning, making lessons more authentic and relevant. Where possible, let students lead the discussion, set the pace, and ask questions that are native to them. Be prepared to spend extra time and adapt to student interests as needed. There is no rush. It's more important that students understand than get through all topics.

Figure 53—Digital Citizenship topics

Digital Citizenship Topics	K	1	2	3	4	5	6	7	8
Cyberbullying	x	x	x	x	x	x	x	x	x
Digital commerce					x		x	x	x
Digital communications				x		x	x	x	x
Digital footprint and Online presence				x	x	x	x	x	x
Digital law				x			x	x	x
Digital privacy				x	x	x	x	x	x
Digital rights and responsibilities	x	x	x	x	x	x	x	x	x
Digital search and research				x	x	x	x	x	x
Fair use, Public domain				x	x	x	x	x	x
Image copyright				x		x	x	x	x	x
Internet safety	x	x	x	x	x	x	x	x	x
Netiquette		x	x	x	x	x	x	x	x
Online Plagiarism				x	x	x	x	x	x
Passwords	x	x	x		x	x		x	x
Social media						x	x	x	x
Stranger Danger	x	x	x						

_____Preview the topics to be sure they're appropriate for your unique student group.

_____Introduce DigCit with Digital Life 101 (available on YouTube).

Cyberbullying

_____Expand last year's discussion with Media Smarts Cyberbullying or Childline Bullying and Cyberbullying. Review statistics in Think Time: How Does Cyberbullying Affect You (search internet for websites).

_____Watch and discuss You Can't Take it Back (search internet for website). What precautions can students take to ensure they are kind and supportive online?

_____If students have blogs, have them post about cyberbullying and comment on classmate posts. Include a compliment, suggestion, or question. Keep the conversation on topic. If your students don't use blogs, post a Discussion question that they can respond to.

_____Circle back on these concepts throughout the year when appropriate.

Digital Commerce

_____What is 'digital commerce' (buying and selling goods online)?

_____How many students have bought something online? If so, did they:

- *check with parents first*
- *verify website was legitimate and secure*
- *feel safe because friends were shopping there*

_____Demonstrate what to look for by using a legitimate site like Amazon.com. Go through process of buying something online:

- *Students must have the money (even with a credit card).*
- *They must provide sensitive information (i.e., credit card number).*
- *Website keeps information and might sell it.*

_____What are the pros and cons of digital commerce? Include:

- *It's easy.*
- *It's private.*
- *Products from other countries are available, even those in conflict with host nation laws and morals, i.e., pornography, illegal music, and other illegal downloads.*
- *Website keeps your private information—or worse, sells it.*
- *Website could be hacked and your financial and personal information stolen.*
- *Website could take your money and provide no product.*
- *Website could steal not only your credit card but your identity. Discuss that.*

_____Consider this scenario: 'Josie' sees a Wii online for $20. She knows that is too cheap. What should she do?

_____What is the best way to be good digital citizens and effective consumers?

_____Circle back on these concepts throughout the year when appropriate.

Digital Communications

_____Digital communications includes:

- *email*
- *IMs/texting*
- *cell phones*
- *chat rooms*

Email

_____Review email etiquette:

- *use proper formatting, spelling, grammar*
- *CC anyone you mention*
- *make 'Subject line' topic of email*
- *answer swiftly*
- *re-read before sending*
- *don't use all caps—THIS IS SHOUTING*
- *don't attach unnecessary files or overuse high priority*
- *don't email confidential information*
- *don't email offensive remarks*
- *don't forward chain letters or spam*
- *don't open attachments from strangers*

_____Why is correct grammar/spelling important in email and not so much with texting? Hint: Consider CCSS.W.7.4: *Produce clear and coherent writing in which development, organization, and style are appropriate to* **task and audience**.

_____Email is often required for online tools. Do students have one? Do they use parents?

_____Discuss 'spam'. What is it? Why is it sent? Cover these:

- *It's a free way to interest people in a product.*
- *Sender earns money on 'click-throughs' (what's a 'click through'?).*
- *It gathers personal information.*
- *It wears receiver down until they finally order.*
- *It spreads viruses that hurt computers (why?).*

_____What should students do when spam reaches their email?

_____When students get an email, follow this simple checklist:

- *Do you know sender?*
- *Is it legitimate? For example, does the 'voice' sound like the sender?*
- *Is sender asking for personal information? Legitimate sources never do.*
- *Is there an attachment? If so, don't open it.*

_____Have students send a well-built email to a classmate (if students have email accounts) and reply to one they receive appropriately.

IM/Texting

_____Discuss texting (article at end of lesson). Watch Jennette McCurdy's "Chicken" Commercial for Safe Kids USA (available on YouTube).

Cell Phones

_____Does school allow cell phones? What are reasons teens should have one:

- *stay in touch with parents*
- *for emergencies*
- *so parents know where they are (via GPS)*
- *to collaborate and share*

_____What are reasons they shouldn't?

_____How many parents try to control cell phone use by:

- *limiting student time on it*
- *limiting the plan*
- *having them share in cost*
- *set up text-free zones, like dinner*

_____Does this work? What would students suggest instead?

_____Discuss student responsibilities with cell phones, including:

- *Don't let them interfere with classwork.*
- *Don't use them for academic dishonesty or cyberbullying.*
- *Don't use them to share inappropriate information.*

_____Watch and discuss Digital Passport Communication Video (available on SchoolTube). Kids who walk with heads down as they text, talk, play games aren't paying attention to their surroundings. This dangerous habit lingers as kids get older and begin to drive.

Chatrooms

_____Here are guidelines for chatting online:

- *parents approve*
- *student shares nothing private*
- *student never meets an online 'friend'*
- *student agrees to leave site and tell an adult if it becomes uncomfortable*
- *student screen name includes nothing linkable to student*

_____Circle back on these concepts throughout the year when appropriate.

Digital footprint

_____If students have Googled their names to find their digital footprint, do it again. Has it changed?
_____Watch and discuss these videos on digital footprints (all available on YouTube):

- *Digital Dossier (footprint)*
- *Digital Footprint*
- *Digital Life 101*

Digital Law and Plagiarism

_____What is **plagiarism**? What can/can't be 'borrowed' from online sites? What are repercussions of 'plagiarism'?
_____Discuss the Common Craft video on plagiarism (available through Common Craft).
_____Discuss copyright law (see poster at end of unit). Using a recent research project, share where students innocently infringed copyrights. What are the consequences?
_____What do students remember from last year's discussion on image copyrights? Some are licensed under Creative Commons, but many have more restrictive licenses. What does that mean? What is the legal way to use an online image?
_____Some want to share their work and collaborate with others. Watch and discuss Wanna Work Together (available on YouTube) about licensing.
_____Now, have students create an image using a school tool or one from Ask a Tech Teacher's resources.
_____When done, share a screenshot on blog/website.

_____Visit blogs of fellow students:

- *Understand their perspective.*
- *Ask questions or respond to comments.*
- *Build on ideas with facts and details.*
- *Follow rules of collegial discussions (see Common Core SL.8.1b).*

_____Circle back on these concepts throughout the year.

Digital privacy

_____Watch and discuss 6 Degrees of Information (available on YouTube). How easy it is to find about anyone through crumbs left online.
_____Discuss what happens to a photo that is shared on social media.
_____Watch Two Kinds of Stupid (available on YouTube).
_____Expand digital privacy discussion to Online Reputations (available at Carnegie Cyber Academy).
_____Discuss using avatars to protect online privacy. For more, see the lesson on *Digital Tools*.
_____Wrap up with a discussion on hacking, the difference between 'hacking' and 'cracking', Black Hat and White Hat. Should kids 'hack' game codes? Is it a victimless crime? What other issues should they consider?
_____Circle back on these concepts throughout the year when appropriate.

Digital rights and responsibilities

_____What are 'digital rights and responsibilities'? Most students come up with 'rights'—access to internet, use of information, documents to be shared, freedom of expression. What are the 'responsibilities':

- *Don't share personal information. Don't ask others for theirs.*
- *Be aware of your cyberspace surroundings.*
- *As in your neighborhood, be kind to others.*
- *If someone is 'flaming' another, help stop it within your abilities.*

_____Watch this Digital Rights and Responsibilities video (available on YouTube).
_____How are online rights balanced by responsibilities?
_____Circle back on these concepts throughout the year when appropriate.

Digital search and research

_____*Discussed in "Internet Search and Research" lesson.*

Fair use, Public domain, Image Copyright

_____*Discussed in "Online Image Legalities" lesson.*

Internet safety

_____Discuss password guidelines and rules. Remind students they never share passwords.

_____Watch and discuss Broken Friendship . (available on YouTube).

_____Ask students how they protect their passwords and online safety when using the Internet.

_____What's the difference between 'http' and 'https'? How important is this level of security?

Netiquette

_____What is '**netiquette**'?

_____Discuss the list of criteria in _Figure 54a_ (full-size poster in the appendix)?

Figure 54a—Netiquette Rules; 54b—Digital pyramid

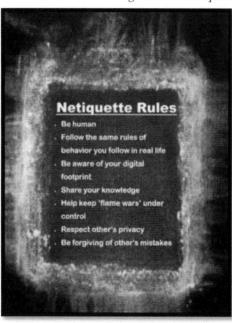

Social Media

_____What is 'social media'? Make sure discussion includes:

- _Facebook and Twitter—social media in general_
- _netiquette_
- _parents_
- _student opinions of social media anonymity_

_____What should be included on a social media profile?

_____What is responsible social media use? Think about digital rights and responsibilities.

_____What are long-term consequences of using/abusing social media? Think back to conversations about cyberbullying,

_____Discuss Teens Talk Back (on YouTube).

_____Discuss **Twitter** and hashtags. Watch Hashtag, You're it! (available on YouTube).

_____Break into groups and discuss social media. What are challenges of so much openness? Then discuss as a class and share thoughts via a blog post or class Twitter feed. Thoughts should be objective with domain-specific language appropriate to the task, audience, and purpose.

_____Circle back on these concepts throughout the year when appropriate.

_____Post the pyramid in *Figure 54b* on the wall in your classroom (full-size poster in appendix). Every time you've discussed a topic, check it off.

_____Wrap up unit with a project that encompasses all areas discussed. Students select presentation/ sharing method. Use any tool discussed in the web communication tools. *Figures 55a-c* are examples (zoom in if needed):

Figure 55a-c—Digital Citizenship projects

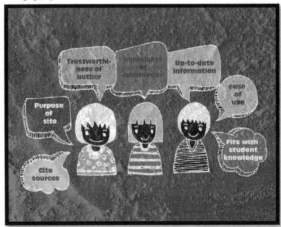

_____When completed, write a post reflecting on what student understands about digcit, why it is important, and how it has affected their personal outlook on internet use.

_____Circle back on these concepts throughout the year when appropriate.

Class exit ticket: ***Tweet on the class Twitter account (or comment on the class blog) about how to stay safe online.***

Differentiation

- *Full digital citizenship curriculum for K-8 available from Structured Learning.*
- *Create a Glogster poster on what it means to be a good digital citizen with links to resources. Include an avatar, a YouTube video, a Tagxedo of digital citizenship words.*
- *Blog about a video watched during unit. Why is it important to be good digital citizens?*
- *Create a map showing where student goes digitally on a daily/weekly basis. Connect locations with 'footprints'.*
- *Create poll on one of the topics above and embed into student blog or wiki. For example, for cell phone use, student might ask classmates to select all that apply:*

  - *I can use my cell any time I want.*
  - *I often use my cell at meals.*
  - *I often use my cell in the car.*
  - *I have a limit on how much time I can spend on phone.*

- *Track and post where students found sources for class research project by placemarking on a world map. This will show how diverse we are in collecting information.*
- *Draw a picture of a digital customer. Make pieces interactive, linked back to products they use and where to find them. Give proper credit.*
- *Debate social media pros and cons. Tape and upload to class website or blog.*
- *Follow Common Sense's Digital Passport with units on cyberbullying, internet search, digital world.*
- *Have a debate on social media pros and cons. Tape and upload to class website/blog.*

"If a man does his best, what else is there?"

- General George S. Patton (1885-1945)

Article 19—Will Texting Destroy Writing Skills

Will Texting Destroy Writing Skills?

Across the education landscape, student text messaging is a bone of contention among teachers. The overarching discussion is texting's utility in providing authentic experiences to students, the type that transfer learning from the classroom to real life. Today, I'll focus on a piece of that: Does text messaging contribute to shortening student attention span or destroying their nascent writing ability

Let's start with attention span. TV, music, over-busy daily schedules, and frenetic family life are likely causes of a student's short attention span. To fault text messaging is like blaming the weather for sinking the Titanic. Texting has less to do with their inability to spit out a full sentence than their 1) need for quickness of communication, 2) love for secrecy, and 3) joy of knowing a language adults don't.

What about writing? In the thirty years I've been teaching everyone from kindergarteners to college, I can tell you with my hand on a Bible that children are flexible, masters at adjusting actions to circumstances (like the clothes they wear for varying events and the conversations they have with varying groups of people). There is no evidence to support that these elastic, malleable creatures are suddenly rigid in their writing style, unable to toggle between casual texting shorthand with friends and a professional writing structure in class.

In general, I'm a fan of anything that gets students writing, and there are real benefits to giving students the gift of textual brevity rather than the stomach-churning fear of a five-paragraph structured essay. I've done quite a few articles on the benefits of Twitter's 280-character approach to writing and my teacher's gut says the same applies to text messaging. Truth, studies on this topic are inconclusive. Some suggest that because young students do not yet have a full grasp of basic writing skills, they have difficulty shifting between texting's abbreviated spelling-doesn't-matter language and Standard English. But a British study suggested students classify 'texting' as 'word play', separate from the serious writing done for class and results in no deterioration in writing skills. Yet another study found that perception of danger from texting is greater than the reality: 70% of the professionals at one college believed texting had harmful effects on student writing skills. However, when analyzed, the opposite was true: Texting was actually beneficial.

It's interesting to note that texting can be a boon to children who struggle with face-to-face situations. These 'special needs' students flourish in an environment where they can write rather than speak, think through an answer before communicating it, and provide pithy conversational gambits in lieu of extended intercourse. In the texting world, socially-challenged children are like every other child, hidden by the anonymity of a faceless piece of metal and circuits.

To blame texting for student academic failures is a cop-out by the parents and teachers entrusted with a child's education. Treated as an authentic scaffold to academic goals, teachers will quickly incorporate it into their best-practices pedagogy of essential tools for learning.

Lesson #9-10 Internet Search and Research

Vocabulary	Problem solving	Homework
• Alt+Tab • Copyright • Creative commons • Domain • Limiters • Plagiarism • Quotes • Refine search • Search bar • Spoof • Toggle	• Browser toolbar gone (F11) • Browser too small (double click title) • Browser text small (Ctrl+) • Web address doesn't work (spelling) • How do I switch between tabs (Alt+Tab) • How do I know if a website is reliable (evaluate, analyze) • It's on Google—it must be free • Doesn't 'fair use' cover me? • This website looks professional (looks can be deceiving)	Keyboard 45 min. 15 min. at a time Review prep; complete digital drawing; watch videos; watch 'War of the Worlds' Blog about search Practice a search
Academic Applications Research, varied academic subjects	**Skills Required** Familiarity with browser used in school	**Standards** CCSS: WHST.6-8.8 NETS: 2b-c, 3a-d

Essential Question

How do I research online, use effective search terms, assess sources, and quote others—while avoiding plagiarism?

Big Idea

Research, remembering the rights and responsibilities of digital citizens

Teacher Preparation/Materials Required

- Have backchannel available.
- Have lesson materials online to preview.
- Have website evaluation sheets (if doing activity).
- Ensure required links are on student digital devices.
- Ask what tech problems students had difficulty with.
- Talk with the grade-level team so you tie into inquiry.
- Integrate domain-specific tech vocabulary into lesson.
- Know whether you need extra time to complete lesson.
- Co-teach with another member of the grade-level team.

Assessment Strategies

- *Previewed required material; came to class prepared*
- *Annotated workbook (if using)*
- *Worked well in a group*
- *Completed research projects*
- *Completed drawing project*
- *Used a wide variety of sources*
- *Understood the importance of website selection*
- *Used good keyboarding habits*
- *Completed warm-up, exit ticket*
- *Joined class conversations*
- *[tried to] solve own problems*
- *Decisions followed class rules*
- *Left room as s/he found it*
- *Higher order thinking: analysis, evaluation, synthesis*
- *Habits of mind observed*

Steps

Time required: **90 minutes or 50 minutes per Google class**
Class warm-up: **Keyboarding on the class typing program**

_____Homework assigned week prior to unit—so students ready for flipped classroom.
_____Any questions from homework? Expect students to come to class with questions.

_____Before beginning, put backchannel device onto class screen.

_____Give students ten minutes to comment on classmate search skills posts (done for homework).

_____Ask: Why research? Encourage students to dig deeper than 'for classwork' or 'to find out something I don't know'. Overarching reasons include to **build and present knowledge.**

_____Common Core requires **the ability to compare, contrast, and synthesize information from multiple sources and share evidence used in student analysis.** Accomplishing this requires students to find and evaluate video clips, websites, and more as sources of information, and differentiate reliable from the alternative.

_____Introduce 'technology advances' with "Did you know?", a video viewed by over 15 million people (available on YouTube).

_____Watch Did You Know 3.0 (available on YouTube) and discuss.

_____Review internet search/research tips:

- *use key words to generate qualified hits*
- *have a general understanding of topic through class discussions, textbooks, or individual interest, as a method of focusing hits*
- *use site extensions to categorize results*
- *pay attention to sidebars, headings, hyperlinks to locate relevant information*
- *use pictures, insets, maps, article links for more information*

_____Discuss essential question: *How do I research online, use effective search terms, and quote others—while avoiding plagiarism?*

_____In this lesson, students will cover four-five activities:

- *internet safety*
- *internet search and research*
- *identify reliable websites*
- *copyrights*
- *summative project I and II*

Internet Safety

_____Review safe internet use. This is covered in detail in the *Digital Citizenship* lesson.

Internet Search and Research

_____If you use Common Sense's Digital Passport, have students play Search Shark.

_____Watch Matt Cutts' *How Search Works* (5.8 million views on YouTube) and discuss.

_____Try Google's series of 50-minute classes called Power Search:

- *how to search*
- *how to interpret results*
- *how to find facts faster*
- *how to check facts*
- *how to put it all together*

_____Have students independently work through lessons (or cover in class if there's time).

_____After reviewing, discuss what students learned.

_____See *Figure 56* for Internet search tips (full size poster in Appendix):

Figure 56—Internet research

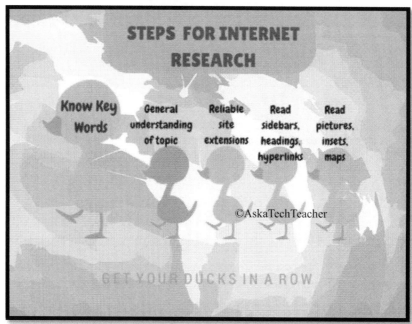

_____Practice with a topic students are discussing in class. For example, type *Winston Churchill*—no quotes—into search bar. Notice the number of hits.

_____Type "Winston Churchill" (with quotes)—you get fewer hits.

_____Type "Winston Churchill" "British Prime Minister"—adding words to refine hits.

_____Type "Winston Churchill" –"World War II"—minus skips sites with words "world war II".

_____How is research different in Word and Google Docs? What about other tools?

_____Discuss how to use online material safely and legally if you haven't covered this topic before (see the lesson on *Digital Citizenship*). Cover 1) citations, 2) copyrights, 3) plagiarism, and 4) digital rights and responsibilities.

_____Circle back on these concepts during year.

Identify Reliable Websites

_____Why is website credibility important? Consider:

- *How can you use websites to locate an answer to a question quickly or to solve a problem efficiently if you don't know website is reliable?*
- *How can you explain an author's reasons and evidence if you aren't convinced they're accurate?*
- *How can you integrate information from several texts knowledgeably if you don't know websites are knowledgeable?*

_____Ask students how they recognize a reliable website when they get that long list of hits on a search page. Disabuse them of the belief that reliability is related to ranking. Focus on two methods to identify reliable websites: 1) extension, and 2) the website itself.

_____Discuss the parts of a website address (see *Figure 57*—zoom in if needed).

Figure 57—What are the parts of a website?

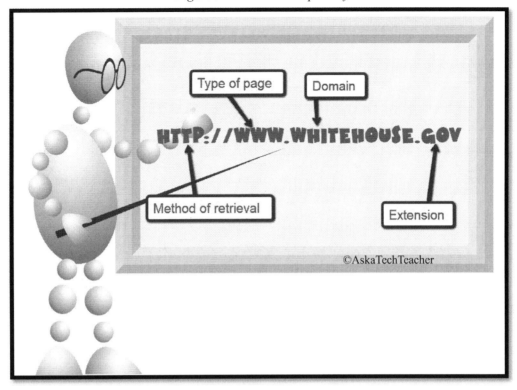

_____Which popular extension is most reliable?

- *.gov—limited to US governmental entities*
- *.edu—limited to educational institutions*
- *.org—used to be non-profit groups.*
- *.net—used to be Internet service providers*
- *.com—most common extension*

_____What can be inferred about reliability from an extension? Does it matter if you're looking for a place to buy backpacks? How about if you're researching hiking?

_____Watch and discuss two videos as a group from the Ask a Tech Teacher resource pages for 'Digital General' or 'Internet Safety'.

_____Demonstrate on class screen how you make decisions about these questions:

- *Is author(s) knowledgeable on the subject?*
- *Is website publisher credible?*
- *Is content accurate based on what students know?*
- *Does content include depth in the topic?*
- *Is information up to date?*
- *Is website unbiased?*
- *Is website age-appropriate? Can students understand verbiage?*

_____Use a variety of sources. Evaluate at least one website using a checklist like:

- o *Common Sense Media*
- o *Cornell University*

Copyrights

_____What do students remember from last year's discussion on image copyrights? Some are licensed under Creative Commons — *Figures 58a-b*:

Figure 58a-b—Creative Commons licensing

_____Many have more restrictive licenses.
_____Watch and discuss A Fair(y) Use Tale (available on YouTube).
_____When must you credit material found online? In general terms, credit the source when using:

- *facts not commonly known or accepted*
- *exact words and/or unique phrase*
- *reprint of diagrams, illustrations, charts, pictures, or other visual materials*
- *opinions that support research*
- *electronically-available media are copy-pasted, including images, audio, video*

_____Copyrights range from public domain to intensely private.
_____Review copyright law (*Figure 59* is a rephrasing—full size poster in Appendix).

Figure 59—Digital law—rephrased

The law states that works of art created in the U.S. after January 1, 1978, are automatically protected by copyright once they are fixed in a tangible medium (like the internet) BUT a single copy may be used for scholarly research (even if that's a 2nd grade life cycle report) or in teaching or preparation to teach a class.

©AskaTechTeacher

_____When searching for images, adjust the search engine to provide only those that are in the public domain. *Figure 60* shows how to find this option in Google:

Figure 60—Copyright protections on browsers

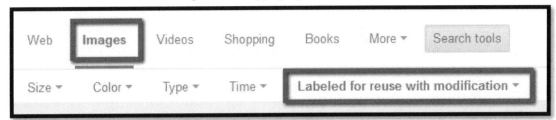

_____Find several images online. Show students how to track them back to their source and then find the copyright protections that are invariably listed on the pages. This is often time-intensive, but necessary: Never assume an image is freely available to use. If students can't find the copyright notice, pick a different image.

_____Discuss how artists share material online. What do these terms mean?

- *Attribution*
- *Non derivative works*
- *Share alike*
- *Non-commercial*

_____Here are two examples of copyrights applied to materials online (*Figure 61*—zoom in if needed):

Figure 61—Two copyrighted images

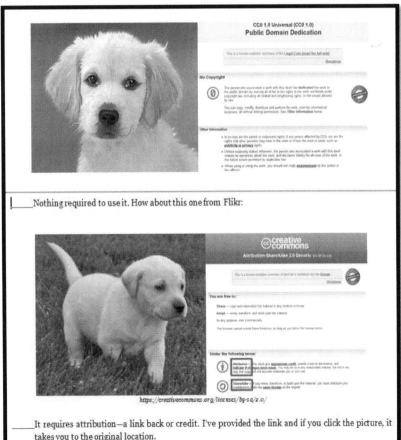

_____Some want to share work and collaborate with others. Watch and discuss *Wanna Work Together* (available on YouTube) about Creative Commons licensing.

_____Discuss how students can find if an image they created is being used online: Drag-drop it into either of these two websites to show all the online sites where it appears:

- *TinEye*
- *Google Images*

_____*Figure 62a* was drawn by a student and posted to her/his public website to share with family and friends. Without her/his knowledge, it was used forty-seven times (*Figure 62b*), not always in places s/he or her/his parents would approve.

Figure 62a-b—Student drawing used without permission

_____What could s/he do in the future? How about add a copyright notice to website, announcing media on the website are protected by copyright laws and cannot be used without permission.

_____Consider the drawing students completed for homework. How would they feel if someone stole it? What if thief posted it online? What if they made ugly comments about it? What if they made money off of it and didn't share it with creator. What if the artist really needed that money to support a family or go to college?

_____Define '**plagiarism**'. Students are familiar with plagiarized text. How does this apply to images, videos, artwork, illustrations, and music?

_____Discuss how to cite a website. Visit EasyBib or Citation Machine.

Hoaxes

_____Discuss how easy it is to fake a picture with programs like Photoshop. Has anyone had this experience? What did they do about that? How did they feel? What were the repercussions?

_____Complete the WebQuest *Hoax or Not* (available on Zunal) and discuss. This puts students in the position of investigating internet scenarios that are presented to viewers as legitimate. The student must evaluate facts and determine if it is a hoax or not. As they do this, they develop skills to help them in their everyday online adventures.

_____Look at *Figure 63*. Did President Roosevelt really ride a moose across a river?

Figure 63—Real or a hoax?

_____In *Figures 64a-b:* Was the tree added to or erased from the original photo? What clues helped students make that decision?

Figure 64a-b: Add or remove pieces from a photo

_____Visit 'Is This Picture Real?'_(available on YouTube or pick one that works for your student group from the Ask a Tech Teacher resource pages). Why do students think it is or isn't real? Why might so many people fall for its message? Note: This website does include some disturbing images. Be careful about allowing students to browse.

_____Visit Zapatopi's Tree Octopus websites. Is it real? How do you know?

_____Discuss as a class whether *Figures 65a-c* are accurate—and how do students know? It's no surprise photos are not accepted as proof in court.

Figure 65a-c—Real or hoax pictures?

_____Show 'War of the Worlds' — a famous video hoax. Discuss how it confused fiction with reality for listeners who missed the first ten minutes. Play it for students from that point.

Summative Project I

_____Students work in groups to research a significant technology advancement of their choice that you have approved (electricity, transportation, communication, computers, internet, etc.).

_____Topic data must be collected from multiple media (video, oral, textual, and images) and include at least one primary source. Evidence will 1) support hypotheses, 2) be well-rounded, 3) demonstrate understanding of topic, and 4) enable students to fully answer question.

_____Students can use the class digital note-taking tool and/or a variety of other methods:

- *copy-paste to a notebook using Word, Google Docs, Notes, or similar. Leave it active on taskbar and toggle (Alt+Tab) between them during research.*
- *snip with Evernote, Snipping Tool, or similar*
- *create audio notes via iPad/smartphone apps*

_____Rephrase saved notes into eighth grade language.

_____Students must include five images:

- *One from a public domain website*
- *One from Google images (that is legal to use)*
- *One they create in MS Word*
- *One they create in Paint, KidPix, or another drawing program*
- *One they create in Photoshop (or similar)*

_____Consider these when preparing project:

- *Who is the target audience?*
- *What is the presentation goal/purpose?*
- *Is all material specifically permitted?*
- *Did all team members participate?*

_____Research done, students share/publish information using an option best-suited to their goals. Consider:

- *a poster using Glogster*
- *a magazine using Canva.com Figure 66b*
- *a website using Google Sites, Weebly, Wiz*
- *a video on YouTube, Vimeo (private channel)*

_____Presentation and project should include:

- *conclusions based on research*
- *reflections based on research (student group opinion)*
- *checklist of one website evaluation*
- *timeline with important events and relevant pictures*

- *people involved in discovery—brief bio, pictures*
- *problems faced and how they were solved*
- *at least one primary source*
- *citations using EasyBib or similar*

Figure 66a-c—Samples of search projects

 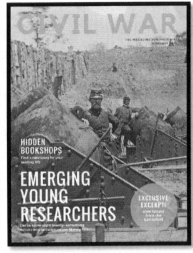 

_____Share/publish in student blog, website, or wiki. Students comment on three classmate posts.

Summative Project II

_____Open school's graphic program (Paint, Google Draw, Photoshop, or another). Have students draw a picture that collaborates with a class discussion (i.e., literature, history, or another).
_____When done, take a screenshot and share on blog/website. Comment on three classmate posts.
_____Conclusion: It's a lot easier to create your own graphics than use someone else's.

Class exit ticket: **Tweet (or comment on class blog) about how student stays safe online.**

Differentiation

- *Have students play 'Search Shark' in Digital Passport.*
- *For more on digital citizenship, follow K-8 Digital Citizenship Curriculum (available from Structured Learn).*

Lesson #11 Word Certification

Vocabulary	Problem solving	Homework
• Attributes • Autocorrect • Endnote • Hyperlinks • Indentation • Mail merge • Quick Parts • SmartArt • Themes • Versions • Views • Wordart	• Doc says, 'read only' (save under a different name) • What's different about save, save-as? • What is today's date? (Ctrl+;) • Can't find doc file (Start-search) • Right-click doesn't work (reboot) • I know the answers, but can't work fast enough on trial tests (make skills habits) • Don't know answer (Google it; use Help files, provided resources, teammates) • How do I add a footer or header? • How do I save as a different filename?	Review notes to prepare for project Watch videos; prepare reflections; complete compare-contrast table and pre-test assessment Keyboard 45 minutes, 15 minutes at a time
Academic Applications research, writing, problem solving	**Required Skills** Intermediate MS Word, self-starter attitude	**Standards** CCSS: CCRA.W.6 NETS: 1d, 3d, 4b

Essential Question

How do I learn enough about word processing to serve my education needs?

Big Idea

Know how to use word processing to produce and publish writing and present ideas efficiently.

Teacher Preparation/Materials Required

- Add Unit and Certification test date to class calendar.
- Have lesson materials online to preview lesson.
- Know whether you need extra time to complete lesson.
- Have student workbooks available (if using).
- Integrate domain-specific tech vocabulary into lesson.
- Ask what tech problems students had difficulty with.
- Know which tasks weren't completed last week.
- Something happen you weren't prepared for? Show students how you fix the emergency without a meltdown and with a positive attitude.

Assessment Strategies

- Previewed required material; came to class prepared
- Worked independently
- Used good keyboarding habits
- Annotated workbook (if using)
- Completed warm-up, exit ticket
- Completed MS Certification test (whether passed or not)
- Joined classroom conversations
- [tried to] solve own problems
- Decisions followed class rules
- Left room as s/he found it
- Higher order thinking: analysis, evaluation, synthesis
- Habits of mind observed

Steps

Time required: *360 minutes or more*
Class warm-up: *Keyboarding on the class typing program*

_____Homework is assigned the week before this unit so students are prepared.
_____Any questions from homework? Expect students to review unit and come to class prepared.
_____Use backchannel program like Socrative to determine student understanding.

_____Any questions on keyboard homework?

_____Define 'word processing'? Name word processing programs (such as Word, Word Perfect, Google Docs, Open Office, Notes, and Text). Why is it important to be able to use them to:

- *Communicate ideas effectively to multiple audiences with a variety of media?*
- *Know what tasks are best suited to word processing as opposed to presentation programs, desktop publishing, or spreadsheets?*
- *Produce/publish writing and present relationships between ideas (Common Core)?*
- *Integrate information from different media to develop a coherent understanding of a topic (from Common Core)?*
- *Write routinely for a range of tasks, purposes, and audiences (from Common Core)?*

_____*Figure 67* is a sample evaluation of the major differences between slideshows, word processing, spreadsheets and the collective category of 'desktop publishing'. This includes a wide variety of tools, not just the four that we usually think of as delivering these goals. For example, 'word processing' includes not just the programs mentioned above, but forums, Discussion Boards, some blogs—any tool that delivers the message primarily with text.

_____You can review these traits or use this table in conjunction with *Figure 68*:

Figure 67—Compare-contrast productivity tools I

Element	Presentation	Word processing	Spread-- sheets	DTP
Purpose	Share a presentation	Share words	Turn numbers into information	Share information using a variety of media
Basics	Graphics-based Design is important to content Layout communicates Few words, lots of images	Text-based Design is secondary to content Layout may detract from words Primarily words communicate	Number-based Focus on tables, graphs Little text; lots of statistics and date Almost no words	Mix of media—equal emphasis on text, images, layout, color
Sentences	Bulleted, phrases	Full sentences with proper conventions	None	Full sentences, bullets,
Content	Slides cover basics, to remind presenter what to say	Thorough discussion of a topic. Meant to be complete document	Statistics, data, charts, graphs	To draw an audience in;
Use	As a back-up to presentation	As complete resource	To support other presentation methods	Good way to group information for easy consumption
Presentation	Speaker presents with their back to the slideshow	Speaker reads from document	Speakers uses it in a presentation or 1:1	Speaker passes out as a handout or take-way
What else				

_____*Figure 68* is an incomplete copy of *Figure 67* that's also in the workbooks (if you're using these). Working with a partner, give students time to complete the blank cells, and then go over the completed copy on the class screen. Would students add any other categories?

Figure 68—Compare-contrast productivity tools II

Element	Presen-tation	Word Processing	Spread-sheets	DTP
Purpose				
Basics				
Sentences				
Content				
Use				
Presentation				
What else				

_____Any questions on preparing for this Certification? The lesson is self-directed. The test will be scheduled at student's convenience.

_____Primary skills addressed are:

- *attributes*
- *auto-correct*
- *comments*
- *endnotes*
- *fonts*
- *footers*
- *footnotes*
- *headers*
- *hyperlinks*
- *images*

- *indentation/tabs*
- *mail merge*
- *navigate and search*
- *page setup settings*
- *protection*
- *Quick Parts*
- *save*
- *shapes,*
- *share documents*
- *SmartArt*

- *spacing settings*
- *spell/grammar check*
- *table of contents*
- *tables*
- *templates*
- *text boxes*
- *themes*
- *versions*
- *Views*
- *WordArt*

_____Here are some test-taking hints:

- *Tests are skills-based and take place in a simulated application environment.*
- *Most questions have multiple tasks; the exam is assessed on outcome and clicks.*
- *Users should be able to locate and utilize key features.*
- *Questions are not worded to be tricky or misleading.*
- *Be well versed in MS Word, persistent in finding answers.*
- *Test takes about 90 minutes.*
- *Skip questions you are not sure of. Return to them at the end of the test.*
- *Keep track of time.*
- *Do not over-think questions.*
- *Stick to the literal.*

_____Students will use as much class time as you can make available to prepare for test using an MS-approved prep website such as:

- *Certiport*
- *Lynda*

_____Training takes approximately five hours. Students can study in groups.

_____Besides class time, students should use homework time to prepare.

_____Before taking certification, students design and take a practice test using a digital tool, such as:

- *Flippity—create Jeopardy-style quiz*
- *PuzzleMaker—crosswords and more (Assessment 17)*
- *StudyBlue*
- *Kahoot—compete in teams*

Assessment 17—MS Word certification study guide

MS Word Certification

```
P A T T R I B U T E S . S T N E M M O C
Y A Q S G N I T T E S G N I C A P S P B
S Y G N A V I G A T E A N D S E A R C H
M H W E M S M . L T S F O O T N O T E S
A J A Q S S E S S K R K T A B Z T . K K
I N P R W E H T N N Z A B A I Y S R X K
L Z O E E A T I A X O L T N B E V T Z N
M D I I P D L U S L E I D R M L C T J P
E V S E T R O R P O P E S E A E E S K V
R N S E E C E C F S N M H R R M T S L P
G , S P X D E C U T E T E R E R S W Z P
E S Y E A O O T A M D T O T A V O J R N
S H R E T N B T O K E C T P M R Z M L Y
M E H E T O I T L R T N K I D S T N O F
S Y G E T O N L X O P C T A N L Z V Z T
D A N A N O E D T E I G R S T G M B Y W
Y T V D M P O U N U T T T N . G S R V Y
S L N E S I A F Q E B J Z Q Z Y Z . T Q
```

_____Have websites on class start page that tie into inquiry for those who finish early.
_____Best practices include:

- *use time wisely*
- *relate certification to college and career opportunities*
- *be self-motivated*

Class exit ticket: ***Take part of a study quiz (like Assessment 17) designed by a classmate. Or fill out the sample in the student workbook (if using).***

Differentiation

- *Extend this Unit to a full grading period, depending upon interest level at school.*
- *Use class digital note-taking tool to collect notes on prep materials for certification exam.*
- *Access free online Word training at GCF Learn.*
- *Practice on MS 360 if available so students get used to taking tests online.*
- *Reflect in blog on achieving MS Certification. Was it important? Did student learn a lot? If they didn't pass, what happened? Student is graded NOT on whether they got certified, but the process followed in pursuing it.*
- *K-8 Keyboard Curriculum available in K-8 Keyboard Curriculum (from Structured Learning).*

Lesson #12 Gradebook and Budget

Vocabulary	Problem solving	Homework
• Absolute reference • Amortize • Discretionary • Format • Formula • Hashtags • If-then • Relative reference • Screencast • Screenshare • Shortkey • Spreadsheet • Tweets • Word processing	• Formula doesn't work (start with =) • When I copy-paste formula, it grabs wrong cells (Consider relative or absolute references) • I can't figure it out (try Help, Google search, ask a neighbor) • This is impossible (use problem-solving strategies discussed earlier) • Numbers are confusing (enhance spreadsheet with images, color) • Spreadsheets are confusing (work with lesson videos) • I don't know what job I want (research and make a choice)	Keyboard 45 min, 15 minutes at a time Review spreadsheet program, videos, how to create a grade book and a budget. Compare-contrast spreadsheets to other tools Bring questions to class
Academic Applications Math, financial literacy, career choices	**Required skills** Working understanding of spreadsheets including completion of at least one project.	**Standards** CCSS: RH.6-8.7 NETS: 1d, 5a-d

Essential Question

How can I use technology to draw conclusions?

Big Idea

Quantitative analysis helps evaluate, and share ideas

Teacher Preparation/Materials Required

- Chat with grade level teachers to tie into inquiry.
- Have preview materials online.
- Have student workbooks (if using).
- Integrate domain-specific tech vocabulary.
- Ensure required links are on student digital devices.
- Know which tasks weren't completed last week.
- Something unexpected happen? Show how you fix it without a meltdown and with a positive attitude.

Assessment Strategies

- *Previewed required material; came to class prepared*
- *Annotated workbook (if using)*
- *Worked independently*
- *Used good keyboarding habits*
- *Completed project*
- *Formulas worked*
- *Completed warm-up*
- *Joined class conversations*
- *[tried to] solve own problems*
- *Decisions followed class rules*
- *Left room as s/he found it*
- *Higher order thinking: analysis, evaluation, synthesis*
- *Habits of mind observed*

Steps

Time required: **90-180 minutes per activity**
Class warm-up: **Keyboarding on the class typing program, paying attention to posture**

_____Homework is assigned before the lesson so students are prepared.

_____Use backchannel program like Socrative to determine student understanding.

_____Any questions from preparatory homework? If students have been following the SL curriculum for a few years, they are prepared. *Figures 69a-c are examples of what they have completed:*

Figure 69a-c——Spreadsheet projects in 2nd-7th

_____Any questions on keyboarding homework?

_____What is a spreadsheet? Name some spreadsheet programs. Why is it important to be able to use them? Prod students for answers that include:

- *communicate information and ideas effectively*
- *present relationships clearly and efficiently (from Common Core)*
- *develop a coherent understanding of a topic or issue (from Common Core)*

_____ Discuss how spreadsheet programs are uniquely qualified to assist in the following:

- *Make sense of problems and persevere in solving them (charts/graphs) Figure 70a:*
- *Reason abstractly and quantitatively (sorting is pivotal to spreadsheets) Figure 70b:*

Figure 70a—Excel formula breakdown; 70b—spreadsheet formulas

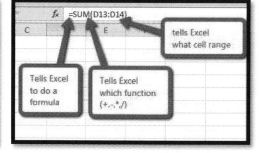

- *Use appropriate tools strategically (spreadsheet is the right tool to share data) Fig.71:*

Figure 71—Spreadsheet chart

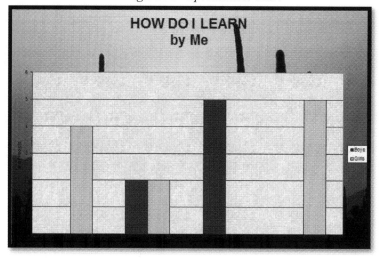

- *Construct viable arguments and critique reasoning of others (quantifiable arguments are defensible and convincing). Based on the formula at the bottom of DQ, what conclusion does Figure 72a reach (Spoiler: Many keyboard faster than handwrite):*

Figure 72a—Formulas in decisions; 72b—model with mathematics with formulas

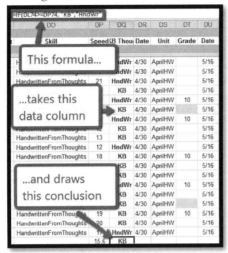 

- *Model with mathematics (i.e., a monthly budget) Figure 72b:*
- *Attend to precision (with a spreadsheet's mathematical properties)—Figure 73:*

Figure 73—Spreadsheet list of formulas

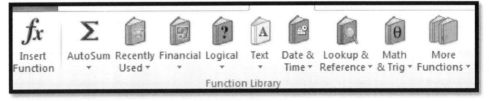

- *Look for and make use of structure (formulas, charts, graphs—Figure 74):*

Figure 74—Spreadsheet data

T2 SPEED QUIZ	WPM	Grade
1	22	9
2	21	10
3	19	6
4	14	8
5	21	8
6	24	8
7	29	10
8	28	10
9	19	9
10	21	10
11	15	8
12	17	10
13	16	10
14	19	10
15	20	10
16	18	10
17	14	10
18	20	10
average	19.83333	9.222222
count	18	18
max	29	10
min	14	6

_____What tasks are better suited to spreadsheets than word processing? Slideshows? DTP? Revisit the compare-contrast chart in the MS Word certification unit. This time, concentrate on how spreadsheets advance communication:

Element	Presentation	Word processing	Spread-- sheets	DTP
Purpose	Share a presentation	Share words	Turn numbers into information	Share information using a variety of media
Basics	Graphics-based Design is important to content Layout communicates Few words, lots of images	Text-based Design is secondary to content Layout may detract from words Primarily words communicate	Number-based Focus on tables, graphs Little text; lots of statistics and date Almost no words	Mix of media—equal emphasis on text, images, layout, color
Sentences	Bulleted, phrases	Full sentences with proper conventions	None	Full sentences, bullets,
Content	Slides cover basics, to remind presenter what to say	Thorough discussion of a topic. Meant to be complete document	Statistics, data, charts, graphs	To draw an audience in;
Use	As a back-up to presentation	As complete resource	To support other presentation methods	Good way to group information for easy consumption
Presentation	Speaker presents with their back to the slideshow	Speaker reads from document	Speakers uses it in a presentation or 1:1	Speaker passes out as a handout or take-way
What else				

_____Have students complete the partial in their workbooks (if using these).

_____Discuss the following Common Core goals and how spreadsheet programs are uniquely qualified to assist in attaining them:

- *Make sense of problems and persevere in solving them (charts/graphs).*
- *Reason abstractly and quantitatively (sorting numbers is pivotal to spreadsheets).*
- *Construct viable arguments (quantifiable arguments are defensible, convincing).*
- *Model with mathematics (i.e., a monthly budget).*
- *Use appropriate tools strategically (When is a spreadsheet exactly the right tool?).*
- *Attend to precision (with a spreadsheet's mathematical properties).*
- *Look for and make use of structure (formulas, charts, graphs).*

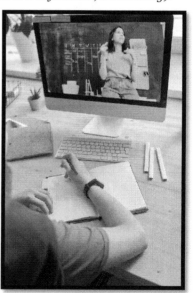

_____Open spreadsheet program (Excel, Spreadsheets, Numbers, or another). Who wants to review layout for class? Inserting data? Creating formulas? Expect students to be able to do this because they reviewed it for homework. Any questions?

_____This lesson includes two projects:

- *create a grading sheet*
- *create a budget of monthly expenses*

Create a grading sheet

_____Students create a grading sheet with formulas that update class grades. Students can format chart to suit their needs (fonts, colors, sizes, fills, classes, borders). All formulas must work.

_____Students use prior spreadsheet training to intuit how to create the chart in *Figure 75*.

Figure 75—Gradebook spreadsheet

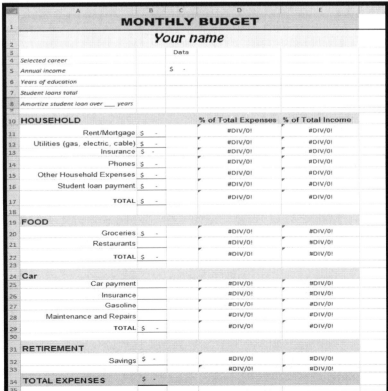

_____When gradebook is completed, have them add grades and watch how it calculates the final grade.

_____What if a grade is weighted? How would they create a formula that would weight the grade?

_____Submit updated spreadsheet weekly.

Create a budget

_____Create a budget for student life after graduating. This will include:

Figure 76—Spreadsheet budget

- *Conclusions*
- *Data analysis*
- *Formatting*
- *Formulas*
- *Grammar and spelling*
- *Headings*
- *Income and expense categories*
- *Personalized information*
- *Relative and absolute addresses (within formulas)*
- *Research*
- *Totals and subtotals*

_____**First**: Choose a career that fits student interests. Start by taking Holland Code Quiz and see what it recommends. There will be several choices. Read about careers, and record 1) job title, 2) annual income, and 3) years of education.

_____**Second**: Virtually visit the college student wants to attend. What does it cost? Use the State College as a default. Multiply annual cost by the number of years required for selected job. For example, if 'Chaplain' (which requires five years of college) and 'University of San Diego' were selected, multiply annual education cost times five. Amortize over ten years on spreadsheet (or the amortization number class agrees on). Divide by twelve (for monthly number) and plug that answer into budget. For this exercise, consider the college loan cost interest-free.

- *Amortize total value of student loan over 10 years. That requires formulas in c8 and b16 (maybe more). Expect students to figure this out with minimal help.*
- *If that is too much of an expense every month, re-evaluate college choice.*
- *If parents are paying for college, plug in costs that student is responsible for only.*

_____**Third**: Plug costs of purchasing a home into spreadsheet based on housing prices in your zip code. Calculate monthly payment (there are lots of calculators online if you don't have one). Plug cost into the spreadsheet. Notice how *#DIV/O!* changes to a number.

- *Under '% of Total Income' and '% of Total Expenses', what does '#DIV/O!' mean?*
- *Click cell D11 and discuss what the formula — =B11/B34 — means (it divides number student came up with for mortgage by 'Total Expenses'). Students find other formulas by themselves.*
- *To come up with the formula, student must pay attention to what EXACTLY they ask the spreadsheet to calculate.*
- *Budget experts recommend that house payment should be no more than 28% of gross monthly income. If this is not the case in the cell for '% of Total Income' allocated to Rent/Mortgage, choose a more affordable house by plugging numbers into spreadsheet until it gives them 28%.*
- *If student can't afford to buy, go to a site like Apartments.com, find an apartment in the preferred zip code and plug rate into budget.*

_____**Fourth**: Choose a Car by using a tool like Auto Trader or CarMax to evaluate choices. Calculate monthly car payment using an online tool and plug the number into budget. As with home payment, budget experts recommend that the car payment not exceed 12% of gross monthly income. If it does, choose a more affordable car. Record the numbers on the spreadsheet.

_____**Fifth**: Calculate and record the remainder of the expenses—utilities, other, phones, groceries, restaurants, insurance, gasoline, other household expenses, retirement. Double check calcs.

_____**Sixth**: Divide Annual Income by 12 to get monthly income. This will enable the student to evaluate whether they are in the 'black' or 'red' for the month.

_____Notice when calculating *% of Total Revenue*, two adaptations must be made to reflect reality. Any thoughts on what that is? How about:

- *Annual income must be divided by 12.*
- *Annual income is not take-home pay. Discuss why. This can be adjusted by multiplying income by 65% (an approximate of the 35% that goes for taxes). Or, have students research how much money goes out in taxes. Use real pay stubs if available.*
- *A working formula might look like: =B11/(C5/12*0.65). Discuss what the dollar sign means, the parentheses, and the .65.*

_____Format worksheet so *money* and *% cells* are reflected with $ and % (use ribbon tools).
_____If student budget is in the red, adjust expenses to get a workable budget.
_____Here's a sample budget (zoom in if necessary for better viewing):

Figure 77—Sample budget

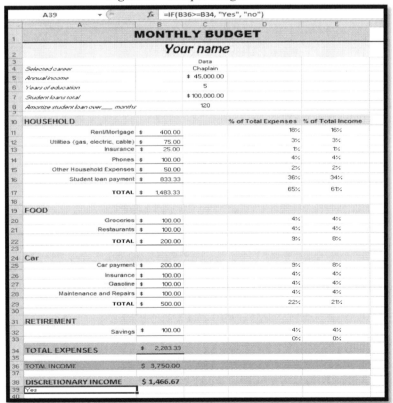

_____Problems? Ask classmates for assistance before going to the teacher. Set up a Twitter #hashtag for Tweets related to project, for example: *#budgethelp* or *#gradebookhelp*.
_____Share work with several classmates. What are their thoughts? Then submit.
_____Have students reflect on what they learned about the usefulness of spreadsheets for evaluating quantitative data. They can post to their blog or tweet to the class Twitter account. Prod them toward answers aligned with Common Core ideas:

- *Spreadsheets facilitate reasoning abstractly and quantitatively.*
- *Spreadsheets facilitate construction of viable arguments.*
- *Spreadsheets aid in making sense of problems and identifying a solution.*
- *Spreadsheets allow for modeling problems.*
- *Spreadsheets use repeated reasoning to solve problems.*

_____Additionally, reflect on:

- *What did they think of the budget?*
- *Any surprises?*
- *How did a spreadsheet program make the evaluative process simpler?*

Class exit ticket: **None.**

Differentiation

- Set up an if-then formula for spreadsheet: **If revenue exceeds expenses, then 'yes' appears in cell. If not, 'no' appears.** How would this be structured? Students can use Help, Google 'if-then formula in spreadsheet, or trial-and-error. [Hint: =IF(B36>=B34, "Yes", "no")].
- Show students how to calculate interest on loans.
- If doing both spreadsheet problems, use the same workbook.
- Have students prepare for and test for Excel certification (see MS Word certification plan).
- Students who finish can start homework—a preview of the next Unit.

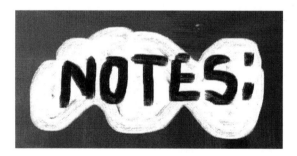

_____

_____

_____

_____

_____

_____

_____

Lesson #13-15 Engineering and Design

Vocabulary	Problem solving	Homework
• Compression • Cross section • Deck • Dynamic load • Elevation • Joints • Load test • Magnitude • Members • Racking • Span • Static load • Structural • Truss	• How do I share in Google? • This is hard (did you go through tutorial first? Are you working with group mates?) • The program froze (look around the screen—is there a dialogue box open?) • Can I download the program at home? (with parent permission—and it's free) • Link doesn't work (Google for address) • Teacher isn't around—I need help (use problem-solving strategies from last unit) • I don't like science—or engineering (think of it as an online game) • My bridge costs too much (check out the $175K bridge video)	View tutorial and how-to videos—become familiar with simulation. Know what group you'll build with Watch bridge videos Keyboard 45 minutes, 15 at a time
Academic Applications Science, engineering, STEM, math, physics	**Required Skills** Basic understanding of online tools, independent spirit	**Standards** CCSS: RST.6-8.7 NETS: 4a, 4c-d, 5a-d

Essential Question

How do I use practical/theoretical knowledge to problem solve?

Big Idea

Precise measurements are critical to many questions.

Teacher Preparation/Materials Required

- Have lesson materials online to preview lesson.
- Know whether you need extra time to complete lesson.
- Have student workbooks available (if using).
- Integrate domain-specific tech vocabulary into lesson.
- Ask what tech problems students had difficulty with.
- Download Bridge Designer to all student digital devices.
- Talk with grade-level team to collaborate on physics, math, geometry, and/or history.
- Know which tasks weren't completed last week.
- Something happen you weren't prepared for? Show students how you fix the emergency without a meltdown and with a positive attitude.

Assessment Strategies

- Previewed required material; came to class prepared
- Submitted bridge project
- Worked independently
- Used domain-specific terms in entry, blog posts, and tweets
- Used good keyboarding habits
- Completed warm-up, exit ticket
- Joined classroom conversations
- [tried to] solve own problems
- Decisions followed class rules
- Left room as s/he found it
- Higher order thinking: analysis, evaluation, synthesis
- Habits of mind observed

Steps

Time required: *270 minutes or more*
Class warm-up: *Keyboarding on the class typing program*

_____Homework is assigned the week before this unit so students are prepared.

_____Use backchannel program like Socrative.

_____Any questions from homework? Expect students to review unit and come to class prepared.

_____Bridge building is an excellent way to update traditional 8th-grade toothpick bridges project.

_____Students will use theoretical knowledge (from research done for homework) in a practical application of building a sample bridge. When done, they will reflect on the importance of both processes (theoretical and practical).

Figure 78—Sample bridge blueprint

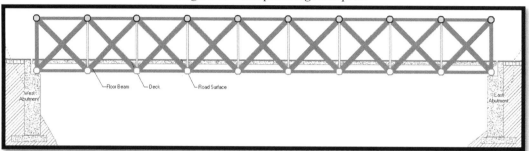

_____Before beginning (for homework), watch videos on bridges and bridge building. If you don't have favorites, check Ask a Tech Teacher's MS resource pages for 'Bridge Building'.

_____Divide students into groups. Give them five minutes to prepare a five-minute presentation on creating an effective bridge, based on homework done to prepare for this unit. Discussions should include bridge size, length, longevity, and cost.

_____When completed, each group will open a bridge design program such as those available from SourceForge, Autodesk, and Bentley. This will be student-directed. You support, not teach.

_____Start with a tutorial, done individually or in groups.

Figure 79a-b—Sample bridge designs

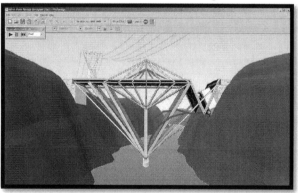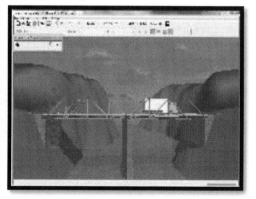

_____Tweet daily about progress, problems, solutions. These are quick, concise, and pithy. Accept difficulties as an opportunity to learn. Use strategies learned in problem-solving unit. Additionally, use Common Core strategies:

- *Use appropriate tools strategically.*
- *Attend to precision.*
- *Make sense of problems and persevere in solving them.*
- *Value evidence.*
- *Comprehend as well as critique.*

- *Understand other perspectives and cultures.*
- *Demonstrate independence.*

_____After bridge is successfully built, save to homework dropbox.

_____Submit contest entry in appropriate category (under 13 or over 13 years old).

_____Use Google Sites, Weebly, Wix, or another website creator to build a project website. Include:

- ○ *explanatory text on design choice and how it worked*
- ○ *screenshots and screencasts of work*
- ○ *insights and analysis*
- ○ *guidance to teach others*
- ○ *facts, definitions, examples, and details*
- ○ *domain specific language. If readers won't know a word, include a glossary*
- ○ *headings, illustrations, charts, graphs, and multimedia useful in understanding the material. This should orient the reader to what is being shared.*

_____Once registered, submit as many designs as student group would like.

_____With a partner, complete the rubric at the end of this lesson.

Class exit ticket: ***Evaluate the design of neighbor using project rubric.***

Differentiation

- *If you live in Mississippi, consider Mississippi Department of Transportation Bridge Building Competition.*

Assessment 18—Bridge building rubric

Engineering/Design Assessment

Project: Bridge Building		Student/Team:			
Pts	**Investigate**	**Design**	**Plan**	**Create**	**Evaluate**	**Group**

Pts	Investigate	Design	Plan	Create	Evaluate	Group
0	Team does not complete work to standard discussed in class	Team does not complete work to standard discussed in class	Team does not complete work to standard discussed in class	Team does not complete work to standard discussed in class	Team does not complete work to standard discussed in class	Team does not complete work to standard discussed in class
1-2	Team states problem/challenge in general terms. Students have difficulty solving building problems.	Team creates a basic bridge design, but it does not satisfy all requirements.	Team struggles to define a plan, understand bridge building concepts that result in a successful bridge.	Team has difficulty building bridge to requirements; is unable to solve all/most problems independently	Team sometimes evaluates problems resulting from their original plan and sometimes cannot solve problems without assistance	Team has difficulty working as a group and remaining positive about problem solving.
3-4	Team states problem/challenge clearly. Team shows evidence of researching topic to solve bridge building problems independently.	Team creates a successful bridge design that is affordable and competitive in the competition. Additionally, they defend in well in blog and tweets.	Team produces a solid bridge building plan that results in a successful bridge and a good contest entry. Adapts theory of bridge building well to practical aspects	Team bridge plan results in a successful bridge that is competitive in the competition. Able to solve all problems using strategies discussed in earlier unit	Team successfully evaluates problems in bridge building design, adapts design to practical applications, and does required research to solve problems.	Team works well as a group, differentiates for team member strengths, and seems to revel in solving problems.
Sub						
Total	©AskaTechTeacher					/20

Lesson #16-18 Learn Through Service

Vocabulary	Problem solving	Homework
• Digital immigrants • Digital natives • Intergenerational • Learning styles • Mash-up • Online meeting • Upload • Virtual • Visual learner	• I explained it, but they didn't understand (try another way) • Not many in class (doesn't matter) • Didn't cover material (doesn't matter) • What should I teach (ask Seniors) • Can't make my group virtual meeting (how do you solve this problem?) • The senior center won't let us upload to their website (find another solution)	Review all notes; know what topics to teach seniors Keyboard 45 min., 15 minutes at a time
Academic Applications research, collaboration, sharing, online safety	**Required Skills** Familiarity with social media, speaking/listening skills, problem solving, keyboarding, digital citizenship	**Standards** CCSS: SL.8.4 NETS: 4a, 4d, 7a-d

Essential Question

How can I share knowledge clearly and efficiently?

Big Idea

Teaching requires presenting in a focused, coherent manner with evidence, sound reasoning, and well-chosen details while using eye contact, adequate volume, and clear pronunciation

Teacher Preparation/Materials Required

- Integrate domain-specific tech vocabulary into lesson.
- Ask what tech problems students had difficulty with.
- Have lesson materials online to preview lesson.
- Know whether you need extra time to complete lesson.
- Talk with grade-level team to tie into conversations.
- Know what topics seniors would like to learn.
- Have a relationship with a local center. Try SeniorNet or Connected Living for local centers.
- Have virtual meeting (Google Hangouts or Skype) how-tos available if needed.
- Know which tasks weren't completed last week and whether they are necessary to move forward.
- Something happen you weren't prepared for? Show students how you fix the emergency without a meltdown and with a positive attitude.

Assessment Strategies

- Previewed required material; came to class prepared
- Used good keyboarding habits
- Completed warm-up
- Joined classroom conversations
- Joined group virtual meetings
- Completed how-to videos
- Received feedback from Center personnel
- [tried to] solve own problems
- Decisions followed class rules
- Higher order thinking: analysis, evaluation, synthesis
- Habits of mind observed

Steps

Time required: **270 minutes or more**

Class warm-up: **Keyboarding on the class typing program**

_____Homework is assigned before this lesson so students are prepared.

_____Use backchannel program like Socrative to determine understanding and required assistance.

_____Any questions from homework? Expect students to review unit and come to class prepared.

_____Have students had any tech problems they'd like to share with the class?

_____**Note:** This project is done as part of 8th-grade community service commitment, in conjunction with other teachers.

_____An important part of 8th grade education is knowing how to speak to a group, listen to feedback, adapt presentation to audience learning style, and communicate information so listeners understand. Nothing makes knowledge more authentic than being able to teach others. This is purposeful learning with real-world application.

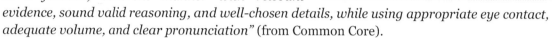

_____In this unit, students will teach a group of seniors how to use technology, *"emphasizing salient points in a focused, coherent manner with relevant evidence, sound valid reasoning, and well-chosen details, while using appropriate eye contact, adequate volume, and clear pronunciation"* (from Common Core).

_____Learning expectations for this unit are:

- *develop and hone the ability to analyze, interpret, and synthesize information*
- *collaborate with others*
- *utilize language skills to present information with the support of technology*

Figure 4--Service learning and CC

_____Discuss how this supports Common Core "Capacities for the Literate Individual":

- *demonstrate independence*
- *build strong content knowledge*
- *respond to varying demands of audience, task, purpose, and discipline*
- *comprehend as well as critique*
- *value evidence*
- *use technology strategically and capably*
- *understand other perspectives and cultures*

"A growing body of research shows that students engaged in high-quality service learning learn to collaborate, think critically, and problem solve. These same deeper learning skills are necessary for students to master the Common Core and meet the expectations of Common Core authors and advocates."

"Linking Service-Learning and Common Core" by Guilfoile and Ryan. 2013

_____Kick this unit off with a guest presentation from a social worker to discuss ways of connecting with an elderly population likely to be somewhat physically infirm. Students learn physical, mental, and emotional characteristics of an aging person and familiarize themselves with problems expected when communicating with the elderly.

_____This intergenerational project focuses on students building community by getting to know elder members. Student become aware of the important roles played by older adults in the community and develop their skills in making connections.

_____Divide students into groups who work together to teach weekly classes to members of a local senior center on how to accomplish specific skills using computers, laptops, iPads, smartphones, digital cameras, and/or other digital devices. Each group will include an adult supervisor.

_____Classes will last 4-6 weeks.

_____Know if the center has laptops/iPads/a computer lab for use. If not, determine how you can bring your own. In either case, bring some digital devices from the school for back-up.

_____Start by introducing student teachers and discussing class goals. Spend time getting to know each other and establishing trust. Set a friendly, open, positive, enthusiastic tone.

_____Ask who has tech problems or subjects they'd like help with. Topics may include:

- *how to use computers—in general terms*
- *use email*
- *use the internet*
- *play online games with grandchildren or each other*
- *use Skype to stay in touch with family*
- *download favorite songs into a music center on their computer*
- *digitize photos to use on phones/desktops/ a desktop slideshow*
- *create blogs to share with each other*
- *create a webcam video to share with family members*
- *read ebooks from an iPad*
- *search for information on areas of interest*
- *solve computer problems (i.e., taskbar disappeared, can't find a program, internet window too small)*
- *tech equipment at senior center that residents don't know how to use*
- *understand domain-specific language associated with technology, i.e., 'cloud'*

Figure 81—How to teach me poster

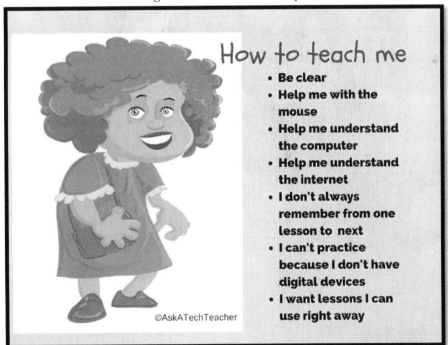

_____Start with an overview of the device being discussed—iPad, laptop, computer. Slowly, carefully. One student presents and the others walk around to help. Always be completely available to seniors—no chatting in groups.

_____Go over computer basics—for example, mouse skills. Make sure seniors understand left/right button, drag-drop, double click. Have online programs available to help them conquer these skills, such as these from SeniorNet.

_____Remember: Olders aren't digital natives, may never have used anything techie, but want to or they wouldn't be in the class.

_____Ask seniors to come to class with a photo they'd like on their computer. Have an iPad app that scans in the photo and makes it available digitally to seniors.

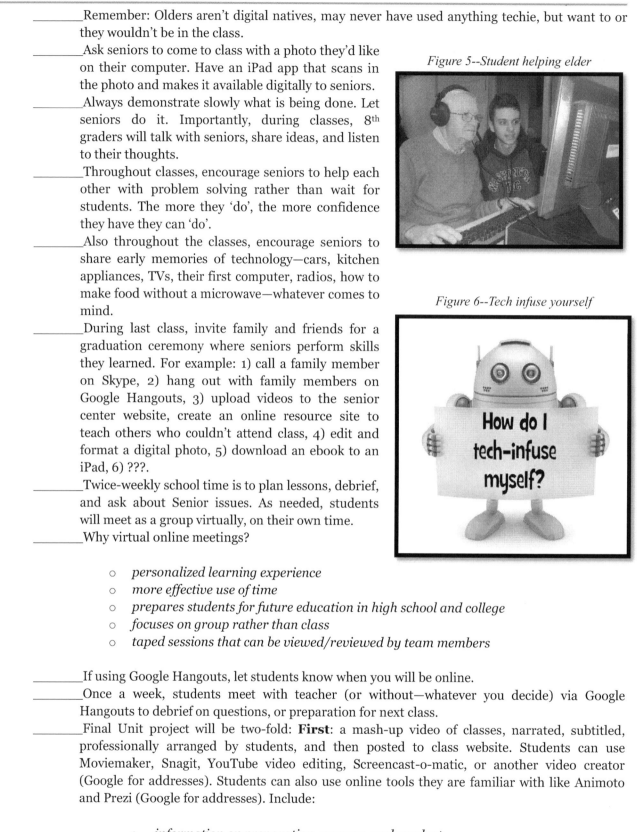

Figure 5--Student helping elder

_____Always demonstrate slowly what is being done. Let seniors do it. Importantly, during classes, 8th graders will talk with seniors, share ideas, and listen to their thoughts.

_____Throughout classes, encourage seniors to help each other with problem solving rather than wait for students. The more they 'do', the more confidence they have they can 'do'.

_____Also throughout the classes, encourage seniors to share early memories of technology—cars, kitchen appliances, TVs, their first computer, radios, how to make food without a microwave—whatever comes to mind.

Figure 6--Tech infuse yourself

_____During last class, invite family and friends for a graduation ceremony where seniors perform skills they learned. For example: 1) call a family member on Skype, 2) hang out with family members on Google Hangouts, 3) upload videos to the senior center website, create an online resource site to teach others who couldn't attend class, 4) edit and format a digital photo, 5) download an ebook to an iPad, 6) ???.

_____Twice-weekly school time is to plan lessons, debrief, and ask about Senior issues. As needed, students will meet as a group virtually, on their own time.

_____Why virtual online meetings?

- o *personalized learning experience*
- o *more effective use of time*
- o *prepares students for future education in high school and college*
- o *focuses on group rather than class*
- o *taped sessions that can be viewed/reviewed by team members*

_____If using Google Hangouts, let students know when you will be online.

_____Once a week, students meet with teacher (or without—whatever you decide) via Google Hangouts to debrief on questions, or preparation for next class.

_____Final Unit project will be two-fold: **First**: a mash-up video of classes, narrated, subtitled, professionally arranged by students, and then posted to class website. Students can use Moviemaker, Snagit, YouTube video editing, Screencast-o-matic, or another video creator (Google for addresses). Students can also use online tools they are familiar with like Animoto and Prezi (Google for addresses). Include:

- • *information on preparation, process, and product*
- • *concrete details, quotes, and examples related to topic*
- • *insights about and analysis of information*
- • *quotes from seniors, students, and care center management*

- *reflections on what went right and wrong*
- *reflection on similarities between peer groups and seniors*
- *domain-specific language*
- *instructions for the next group of 8th graders planning to take this Unit with a goal of helping them understand project*

Figure 7--Student quote on teaching elders

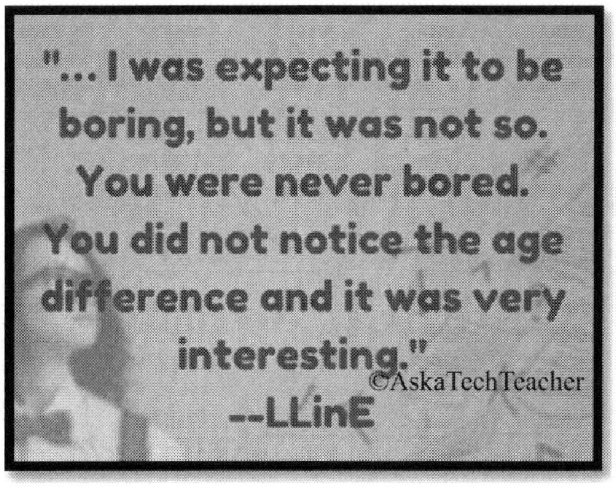

"... I was expecting it to be boring, but it was not so. You were never bored. You did not notice the age difference and it was very interesting." --LLinE

©AskaTechTeacher

Students will shoot video, write copy, and edit themselves.

_____**Second**: create a how-to library of videos for the senior center; upload to their website.

Class exit ticket: ***None.***

Image credit: Knowledge Volunteers Project and European Lifelong Learning Magazine

Differentiation

- *For more information on Common Core Standards and Service Learning, read "Linking Service Learning and the Common Core Initiative"*
- *Click LearnToGive.org for more intergenerational projects*

Lesson #19-21 Visual Learning

Vocabulary	Problem solving	Homework
• Font • Gardner • Infoactive • Infogr.am • Infographic • Layout • Multiple intelligence • Piktochart • Tweeple • Tweets • Type • Visual appeal • Visual learner	• Browser toolbar disappeared (try F11) • Browser window too small (double click title bar) • My browser text is too small (Push Ctrl+ to zoom in) • How do I search internet (type into search or address bar) • How do I add keywords (use + or –) • Can't find copyright (try bottom of website) • It's difficult toggling between sources to compare/contrast (Alt+tab) • How do I select a visual	Keyboard 45 minutes, 15 minutes at a time Review prep material; watch all videos; take poll Prepare to discuss Gardner's Intelligence. Take 1-2 of the learning style quizzes

Academic Applications	Skills Required	Standards
Research, varied academic subjects, learning	Familiarity with problem solving, keyboarding, digital citizenship, graphic organizers	CCSS: W.8.6 NETS: 1b, 3d,

Essential Question

How do I use technology to communicate as a visual learner?

Big Idea

Students use visual communications to share ideas in a clear, succinct fashion

Teacher Preparation/Materials Required

- Have backchannel available.
- Coordinate with co-teacher.
- Have lesson materials online to preview.
- Have website evaluation sheets (if doing activity).
- Ensure required links are on student digital devices.
- Ask what tech problems students had difficulty with.
- Talk with grade-level team so you tie into inquiry.
- Integrate tech vocabulary into lesson.
- Know if you need extra time to complete lesson.

Assessment Strategies

- Came to class prepared
- Annotated workbook (if using)
- Worked well in a group
- Showed creativity
- Created/shared infographic that met requirements
- Created blog post
- Commented on class posts
- Used good keyboarding habits
- Completed warm-up, exit ticket
- Joined class conversations
- [tried to] solve own problems
- Decisions followed class rules
- Left room as s/he found it
- Higher order thinking: analysis, evaluation, synthesis
- Habits of mind observed

Steps

Time required: **270 minutes, or 50 minutes per Google class**
Class warm-up: **Keyboarding on the class typing program**

_____Homework assigned week prior to unit—so students ready for flipped classroom.
_____Any questions from preparatory homework? Expect students to review upcoming unit and come to class with questions.

_____Use backchannel program to determine student understanding and where to offer assistance.

_____What does it mean to organize ideas visually rather than textually? Hint: It's more than pictures. Think of examples completed in past (*Figures 85a-d*):

Figure 85a-d—Visual learning projects

 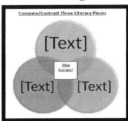  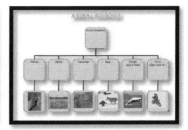

_____What's the difference between sharing via 'text' and 'visually'? Can both be blended to make a more effective message? In *Figure 86b*, each spot on the Thinglink image goes to information like the text in *Figure 86c* and the image in *Figure 86a*:

Figure 86a-c—Thinglink hotspots

_____This lesson includes four sections:

- *background on learning styles*
- *background on visual learning*
- *infographics*
- *summative project*

Background on learning styles

_____Divide class into groups. Give them five minutes to organize thoughts on a topic below:

- *Discuss learning styles—logical (mathematical), visual, linguistic, kinesthetic, musical, interpersonal intrapersonal, naturalistic, and existential. This can be discussed anecdotally by students. Personal experiences are fine.*
- o *How might a visual organizer (like those done in prior years if you've been using the SL technology curriculum):*

  - *build content knowledge*
  - *use digital media strategically*
  - *help students understand other perspectives and cultures*

o   *Discuss what it means to organize ideas visually rather than textually? Hint: It's more than pictures. Think of examples completed in the past. What's the difference between sharing via 'text' and 'visually'? Would blending both be more effective?*
o   *What does Gardner's Multiple Intelligences (reviewed for homework) mean (Fig. 87)?*

Figure 87—Learning styles

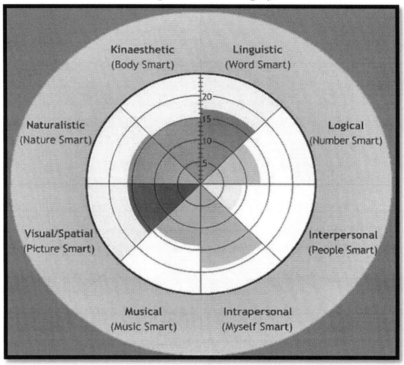

_____Each group presents their thoughts to classmates, using agreed-upon rules for speaking and listening. Allow questions.

_____Why discuss learning styles with students? Why is that important in their educational journey?

_____Discuss the survey(s) students took for homework similar to:

- *Edutopia's quiz*
- *North Carolina State University's learning style quiz*

Figure 88a-b—-Learning style quizzes

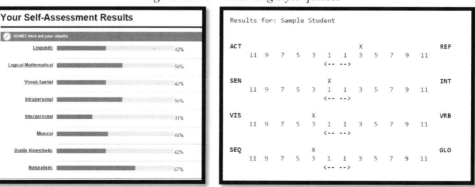

_____Have students take a poll (created in Google Forms, PollDaddy, or another) on what type of learner they are (based on Gardner's Multiple Intelligences and learning style quizzes):

Figure 89a—Learning style poll in Google Forms; 89b—PollDaddy

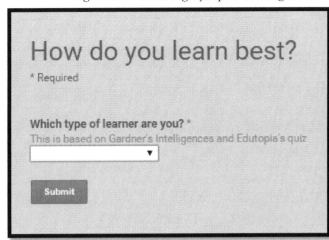

Background on visual learning

_____In 7th grade, students completed projects in all these learning styles. This year, students will concentrate on visual learning. *Figures 90a-e* are examples used between kindergarten and 7th grade (if students have followed the SL technology curriculum):

Figure 90a—Visual organizers in 2nd grade; 90b—3rd; 90c—4th; 90d—6th; 90e—7th

_____Discuss concept of organizing ideas visually rather than textually. What's the difference between sharing via 'text' and 'visually'? Why is a blend of both more effective?
_____Visual learning includes desktop publishing, art, graphic organizers, and infographics. In prior years in the SL curriculum, students have spent time on each of these (*Figures 91a-c*):

Figure 91a-c—Visual learning projects

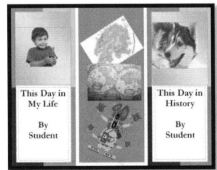

_____This year, we focus on infographics.

Infographics

_____Discuss infographics (a visual and linguistic representation of data) and how they:

- *build strong content knowledge via visual media*
- *respond to varying demands of audiences*
- *use technology and digital media strategically and capably*
- *help understanding of other perspectives and cultures*
- *address the needs of different audiences*
- *are appropriate to varied audience, task and purpose*
- *encourage students to interact and collaborate*

_____Why are they NOT like the graphic organizers students created in *Figures 91a-c*?

_____Infographics are popular because they sum up great volumes of information that would take a reader hours to process. Layout and visual appeal are as important as information summarized.

_____Before continuing, review use of internet images (in-depth discussion in lessons on *Digital Citizenship* and *Internet Search and Research*). Discuss how students can make their own graphics (in Paint, Photoshop, GIMP, KidPix, or another art program) rather than risk infringing someone else's rights.

_____In *Figures 92a-c*, how does the layout make you want to look closer?

Figure 92a-b—Sample infographics in Hubspot; 92c—Piktochart

 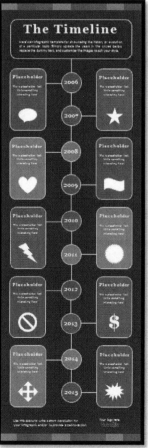 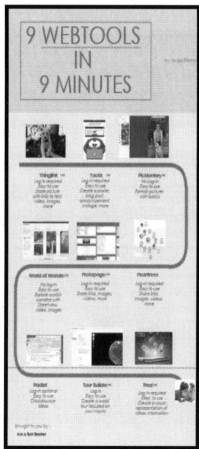

Credit for Figures 92a-b: Hubspot

_____Take as much time as necessary to answer questions. This is an important and authentic topic.

Summative Project

_____Working in groups, students select a topic that supports class inquiry. Alternatively, all groups could create infographics on the same topic.

_____Data will include information student has learned already on the topic—they will not research. This is an opportunity to share knowledge. Exception: Students can take 'a few' minutes to verify data they wish to include. This could include:

- *facts*
- *figures*
- *essential opinions*
- *organic information*
- *primary sources*

_____Students create an infographic using a template of your choice. Possible choices:

- *Canva – Figures 93a-b*
- *Easel.ly*
- *Infogr.am*
- *Piktochart — Figure 92c*

Figure 93a-c—Infographics

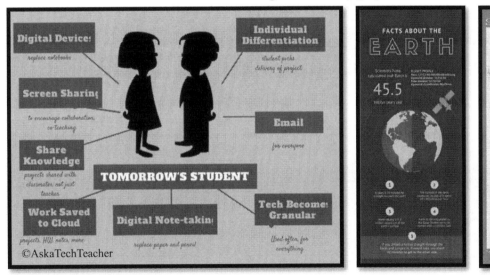

Figure 93c: Credit— Writing Rocks

_____When done, students share their infographic with class and discuss:

- *attractiveness of display*
- *use of color, fonts, and layout to share information*
- *accuracy and relevance of information*
- *use of multiple sources*
- *selection of credible sources*
- *use of academic and domain-specific language, in words understood by 8th graders*
- *citations where needed*

_____Insert into a blog post and explain why student feels their infographic represents the topic.

_____Comment on posts of three other groups and discuss where students feel the infographic of that group fulfills/fails to fulfill requirements. Remember agreed-upon rules of discussion (which also apply in a social media forum like blogging):

- *be respectful*
- *comment to build the conversation, not judge*
- *express ideas clearly*
- *build on ideas of others*
- *make relevant observations*
- *keep discussion on topic*
- *acknowledge new information*
- *use domain-specific language*

_____Continually throughout class, check for understanding.

Class exit ticket: **Review the results of the learning style poll. Tweet (or post a comment to a class Discussion Board) what learning style is most prevalent among your classmates.**

Differentiation

- *Instead of an Infographic, students can create a Prezi or a Glogster if they haven't used these programs before. Goal remains the same: Educate readers visually.*
- *Discuss body language. Show how much you can tell about students by their hands, facial expressions, and body movements. Provide concrete examples, such as:*

  o *What does it mean when a person is quick to giggle?*
  o *What does it mean when someone looks up and to the left?*
  o *What does it mean when someone fidgets as they talk?*

- *Present completed infographics to class via class screen.*
- *Students who finish can start homework preview of next unit.*

Lesson #22-24 Robotics

Vocabulary	Problem solving	Homework
• Angle beams • Bevel gear • Block • Clutch gear • Debug • Driver gear • Forever loops • Gear teeth • Idler gear • Input axle • Loops • Output axle • Pegs • Rigid construction • Robotics • Spur gear • Ultrasonic sensor • Worm gear	• Website address won't link (push spacebar after address). Still won't work (does it start with 'http://'?) • What does 'Save early-save often' mean? (Ctrl+S often to save data) • How do I *** (try different strategies) • Program doesn't work. (debug. Go through all steps to find mistake) • I like building robots but not other stuff • My teammates aren't working as hard as I am (review agreed-upon rules for working in groups) • I have to run back-and-forth to computer and robot for instructions (use iPad) • I've tried all year and still don't type fast (use all fingers, eyes on screen) • Why learn robotics? I don't like Legos (think problem solving, critical thinking)	Be prepared to discuss robotics. Review notes on project; watch all videos; prepare reflections Be prepared to discuss CC and robotics Review Asimov's Laws of Robotics; know favorite robots Keyboard 45 minutes, 15 minutes at a time

Academic Applications	Required Skills	Standards
Math, science, engineering, STEM, STEAM	Familiarity with problem solving, coding, keyboarding, digital citizenship	CCSS: Math.Practice.MP NETS: 4a-b, 5c-d

Essential Question

How does technology make life better (and what is 'better'?)

Big Idea

Technology enables me to control devices that make life easier

Teacher Preparation/Materials Required

- Talk with grade level team so you tie into inquiry.
- Integrate domain-specific tech vocabulary into lesson.
- Have lesson materials online to preview lesson.
- Know whether you need extra time to complete lesson.
- Have student workbooks available (if using).
- Ask what tech problems students had difficulty with.
- Know which tasks weren't completed last week.
- Something happen you weren't prepared for? Show students how you fix it without.

Assessment Strategies

- Came to class prepared
- Teacher signed off challenge.
- Checked points of reflections on each challenge, problem ID.
- Kept blog posts updated with progress reports and reflections.
- Solved most of group problems without teacher assistance.
- Final project; journal and video.
- Completed warm-up, exit ticket
- Decisions followed class rules
- Left room as s/he found it
- Higher order thinking: analysis, evaluation, synthesis
- Habits of mind observed

Steps

Time required: **360 minutes or more**
Class warm-up: **Keyboarding on the class typing program**

_____**Homework is assigned the week before this unit so students are prepared.**

_____Any questions from homework? Expect students to review unit and come to class prepared.

_____Any tech problems to share?

_____Use backchannel program to determine student understanding and where you might offer assistance.

_____Why learn 'robotics? Consider 7th grade robotics. If that isn't available, discuss what students know from personal experience. Prod students to come up with:

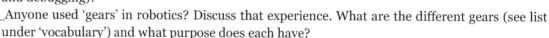

- *thinking skills*
- *problem-solving skills*
- *critical thinking*
- *application of learned math*

_____What part of robotics contributes to each of these areas (i.e., learning to program, building sensors, and debugging)?

_____Anyone used 'gears' in robotics? Discuss that experience. What are the different gears (see list under 'vocabulary') and what purpose does each have?

_____In this lesson, students will evaluate how different Lego gears work. Grading is based on **blog posts, tweets, and labeled drawings.**

_____Pre-assessment: Working in groups, create a sketch (small details are not needed) then describe possible functions of different gears (see 'gears' resources under 'Extension' at end of Unit). Post this as an image to class Twitter account or to student blog.

_____Common Core Standards for Mathematical Practice traits to succeed in math are about more than math. They are fundamental to daily decisions—*evaluate new circumstances and determine a direction, consider possible paths to an end and select the most likely to succeed, mull over new ideas and fit them into accepted constructs.* These are best taught as part of a larger process like robotics, Alice, and Sketch-up.

_____Discuss the meaning of:

- ***Make sense of problems and persevere in solving them***—*robot does what it is told. Students identify problem, find programming error, and fix it.*
- ***Reason abstractly and quantitatively***—*symbol-based program requires an abstract understanding of what is occurring and an ability to visualize results.*
- ***Construct viable arguments and critique reasoning of others***—*if script fails to achieve desired results, critique process. Help neighbors who are stuck.*
- ***Model with mathematics***—*debugging scripts is like decoding math formulae.*
- ***Use appropriate tools strategically***—*robotics requires a plethora of scripts, blocks, tools. Adapt them strategically.*
- ***Attend to precision***—*'garbage in garbage out'—for the program to accomplish what students want requires precision.*
- ***Look for and make use of structure***—*look at available tools, scripts, blocks, options, and select those that facilitate student needs*
- ***Look for and express regularity in repeated reasoning***—*notice when a formula/program/script repeats itself (and use Forever Loop).*

_____Goals of this unit include build off of the basic understanding of robotics learned in 7ᵗʰ grade:

- *How do gears help the work of a robot?*
- *How do we program the robot?*
- *How do we problem-solve if/when robot doesn't work correctly?*
- *How do we work collaboratively in accomplishing a common goal?*

_____Tasks student groups will be expected to accomplish:

- *complete a series of challenges*
- *document and reflect on findings, problems and resolutions*

_____Teaching strategies:

- *Students receive feedback during each challenge including building adjustments, programming tweaks and creative suggestions.*
- *Students have video tutorials and simulations to guide them.*
- *Students work at their own pace.*
- *Assessment comes from student documentation and reflection rather than subjective 'successes.*

_____Don't be surprised if students come up with questions you don't know the answer to. The joy of tech is exploration—finding answers to new questions. Remind students **this is fun**, and they should not be surprised if they must:

- *improvise*
- *change the rules*
- *try things they don't know the answer to*

_____In fact, you want this to happen.

_____Before beginning, discuss: What are robots? What are their uses? Write answers on class screen as class brainstorms.

_____Discuss Asimov's Laws of Robotics:

- *A robot may not injure a human being, or through inaction, allow a human being to come to harm.*
- *A robot must obey the orders given it by human beings except where such orders conflict with the First Law.*
- *A robot must protect its own existence as long as protection does not conflict with the First or Second Law*

_____Why are robots appealing? Discuss popular robots like:

- *7 of 9 (Borg in Star Trek)*
- *Bomb Disposal robots*
- *C-3PO and R2-D2*
- *Daleks (from Dr. Who)*
- *Data (from Star Trek)*
- *Consumer robots*
- *I, Robot (Asimov)*

- *Industrial robots*
- *Lost in Space robot*
- *Mars Curiosity*
- *Marvin the Paranoid Android*
- *Mining robots*
- *Tin Man (Oz)*
- *Transformers*

_____Discuss how robot knows what to do. How do humans know? Animals? The computer? What's the difference between a 'sentient' being and one that is 'non-sentient'? Anyone see Matrix?

_____Show a sample robot students will build and the main parts (see *Figure 94a*):

- *movable physical structure*
- *sensors*
- *gears*
- *power supply*
- *brain*

_____Pick a theme authentic for students, such as NASA's Mars lesson plan (available at NASA website). Students create their version of Curiosity and explore the Red Planet, showing how gears make this more efficient and effective.

_____Place students in groups. Pass out parts box (see *Figure 94b*). Review. Let students play without mixing them up.

Figure 94a-b—Robotic pieces

_____Review robotics user guide. If students have iPads, load guide into iBooks or Kindle (or similar reading app). Review intro, software, technology, parts list, building guide.

_____Demonstrate how to build a basic robot by reading directions and identifying required parts and then let students do this.

_____This robot isn't sentient, so will only do what it's told. Students do so by programming.

_____Give students time to review programming software (such as Lego Mindstorm Education NXT Programming in *Figures 95a-b*). Encourage them to test all menu items, try simple programs to see what happens, and read help files. This is fun if students are more geek than engineer.

Figure 95a-b—Robotics programming

 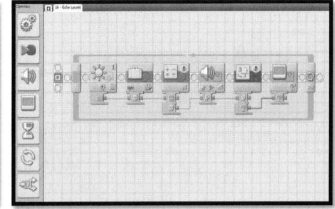

_____Create a sample program along with students (see *Figure 95b*). Compare it to Algebraic expressions students work with in math.

_____Demonstrate how to upload program to robot (see *Figures 96a-b*).

Figure 96a-b—Finding robot program

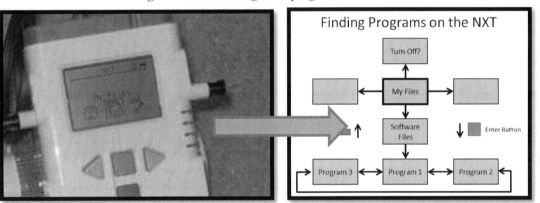

_____Have students program their basic robot to climbing a slope. Discuss what will be required to accomplish this in hardware and programming and then let students work as you observe.

_____That done, students work together to accomplish six tasks:

- o *reverse directions*
- o *accelerate*
- o *turn*
- o *climb various ramps quickly*
- o *detect sound*
- o *detect touch*

_____These tasks must use parts such as:

- o *forklift arm*
- o *karate arm and chopping block*
- o *kicker and long arm*
- o *pusher*

_____Here are 'gears' resources (might have to be adapted to class resources and goals):

- o *climbing using gears*
- o *video about gears*
- o *gear basics*
- o *speed up with gears*

Figure 97a-b—Completed robots

_____Throughout robotics, students use digital note-taking tool to capture data, screenshots and screencasts of work, digital cameras, and traditional videos (taken via iPad or smartphones).

_____Throughout robotics, expect students to blog about their efforts. What works? What problems do they encounter? Get help from school blogger community. Take pictures and videos of what they're doing and share. Include labeled drawings to clarify student work. Use poster and drawing webtools students have been introduced to through this curriculum. Comment on posts of others. Answer questions. Applaud successes. Follow class discussion rules.

_____Throughout robotics, students tweet out their progress through the class Twitter account and proscribed #hashtags, i.e., #robotgears, #hillclimbing.

_____When a group thinks they have completed a task, they have three tries to demonstrate to teacher.

_____There are two Final Challenges. Pick one:

_____**First**: Bot Battles:

_____Students create a program for the sole purpose of pushing an opponent out of a masking-tape ring created on carpet. Use tools practiced so far—climbing, reversing directions, and accelerating. Place two robots inside ring. Start programs and see what happens.

Figure 98a-b—Bot Battles

_____**Second**: Climbing Battles:

_____Write a hill climbing program. Put two programmed bots at the base of a ramp and see whose robot can beat the other robot to the top.

_____In both Final Challenges, success is highly dependent upon robot's construction. Discuss what elements might make a robot more/less successful. When a team's bot races and loses, observe what caused it and adjust bot to be better and smarter.

_____Use Tournament Elimination poster at end of unit to track Challenges. It's created in a spreadsheet (column/row designations are included so you can reproduce if desired).

Figure 99—Tournament elimination poster

_____If students have workbooks, they can keep track of team progress.

_____If desired, award certificates (sample at end of lesson). Ideas include: Best Sportsmanship, Most Creative, Best Bumper Elimination Race (bump the other bot off the hill climb), Slowest Hill Climb (without stopping) at 60 degrees, Fastest Hill Climb at 30 degrees, Fastest Hill Climb at 45 degrees, Best Obstacle Course Hill Climb (put objects in the way). The teacher can determine winner or have students vote by secret ballot.

_____Best practices for robotics include:

- *Don't share robots. Each group has their own.*
- *If a robot doesn't do what you thought it would, re-evaluate and try again.*
- *Post and review class rules.*
- *Watch group dynamics and head off potential problems.*
- *Clean up as you work. Model this during activities. Allow plenty of clean up time.*

Class exit ticket: **Review the program created by a neighbor. Is it like yours? Did s/he get to the same result in a different way?**

**Image Credit: Dave at NxtPrograms.com
*** Lesson collaboration: Thanks to Rich Linville at Teachers Ask

---

Differentiation

- *For introductory robotics training materials, visit Carnegie Mellon's NXT Video Trainer.*
- *Don't want to use Lego Mindstorm? Try Microsoft Robotics.*
- *If robots use ultrasonic sensor, they might interfere with each other. Be aware of this.*
- *Pick one of 14 options on NASA's Mars Education website to engage students.*
- *Enter a robotics competition as a school team.*
- *Ask students to analyze how robots know what to do. How do they know where they are? How do they know where to go? How do they control their 'bodies'? How might they see the world? (from Carnegie Mellon grad student David S. Touretzky's paper, "Seven Big Ideas in Robotics, and How To Teach Them")*
- *Watch MakerBot and Robohand on using 3dPrinting a Robots to create a mechanical hand. This is the story of an individual with a belief that he could solve problems.*

Assessment 19—Team Elimination Poster

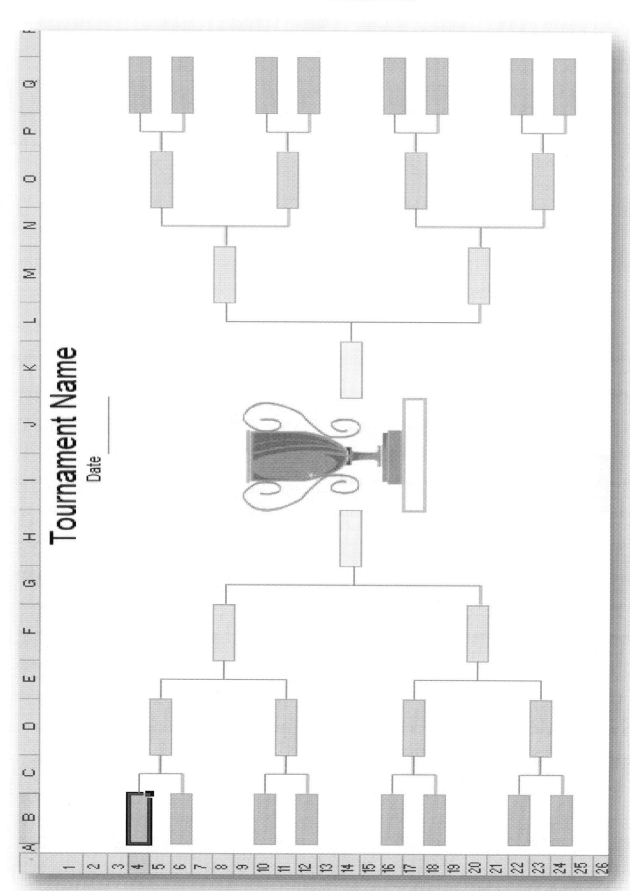

Assessment 20—Robotics certificate

Lesson #25-27 Programming with Alice

Vocabulary	Problem solving	Homework
• Arrays • Class • Color • Debug • Events • Method • Object • Opacity • Parameters • Properties • Variables • World	• I can't understand how to *** (Check resources, Help, neighbors) • I can't remember how I *** (check scripts where you did this before) • How do I add objects? • How do I move the camera around? • I tried—and failed—to install Alice at home (check hardware is compatible) • My Alice world wouldn't load (where did you save it? Did you back it up?) • Audio file won't play (will Alice play another audio file, i.e., .wav)	Watch all videos included in lesson Review project prep and Alice rubric Test Alice on class computer or home Keyboard 45 minutes, 15 minutes at a time
Academic Applications Math, science, engineering, STEM, STEAM	**Required Skills** Facility with computers and online tools, an inquirer's approach to learning	**Standards** CCSS: Math.Practice.MP NETS: 4a-b, 5c-d

Essential Question

How can math be creative and collaborative?

Big Idea

Learn mathematical/computational ideas by creative thinking

Teacher Preparation/Materials Required

- Make sure Alice is on all computers.
- Tie Alice into problem solving unit earlier.
- Integrate domain-specific tech vocabulary into lesson.
- Have lesson materials online to preview lesson.
- Know whether you need extra time to complete lesson.
- Have student workbooks available (if using).
- Talk with grade-level team to tie into inquiry.
- Co-teach Alice with another grade-level team member.
- Something happen you weren't prepared for? Show students how you fix it with a positive attitude.

Assessment Strategies

- Came to class prepared
- Completed tutorial
- Completion of Alice world
- Created summative rubric
- Worked independently
- Used good keyboarding habits
- Completed warm-up
- Joined classroom conversations
- [tried to] solve own problems
- Decisions followed class rules
- Left room as s/he found it
- Higher order thinking: analysis, evaluation, synthesis
- Habits of mind observed

Steps

Time required: *360 minutes or more, spread throughout the school year*
Class warm-up: *Keyboarding on the class typing program*

_____Homework is assigned the week before this unit so students are prepared.

_____Any questions from homework? Expect students to review unit and come to class prepared ready to ask questions, if needed.

_____Any tech issues to share with the class?

_____Use backchannel program like Socrative to determine student understanding and where you might offer assistance.

_____Resources useful in unpacking Alice in your classroom include (available on YouTube):

- *Piloting Alice in the Upper School by Middle School students*
- *Duke University's Alice 'Getting Started' videos are here*
- *list of Alice Common Core standards (from Duke University School of Education)*

_____If you don't want to use Alice, try one of these or another listed in the Ask a Tech Teacher resource pages:

- *Code Monster*
- *Hakitzu*
- *Khan Academy Computer Science*
- *Gamemaker*

_____Discuss 'I Like Programming' (*available on YouTube*)—over 15 million hits.

_____Divide class into groups. Give them 5 minutes to collaborate, and then each shares a summary, analysis, and thoughts about one video they watched. Take questions.

Figure 100a-b—Class using Alice

_____'Programming' is the buzzword among middle school students. They either want to do it or are afraid of it. What does 'programming' mean? Who has their own website? Who wants to write programs and/or apps? Discuss how programming promotes problem-solving, critical thinking, and computational thought.

_____Common Core Standards for Mathematical Practice can be tied into Alice

- ***Look for and express regularity in repeated reasoning***—*notice when a formula/program/script accomplishes a particular task and continue to use it for that purpose (Figure 106b):*
- ***Make sense of problems and persevere in solving them***—*Alice worlds do only what they are told to. You must know where you made a programming error and fix it.*
- ***Reason abstractly and quantitatively***—*Alice programs two-dimensionally. To visualize process requires an abstract understanding of what is occurring (Figure 102b):*

Figure 102a—Make sense of problems; 102b—reason abstractly

- **Construct viable arguments and critique the reasoning of others**—*Be open to criticism and work collaboratively to accomplish goals (Figure 103):*

Figure 103—Construct viable arguments (in Alice)

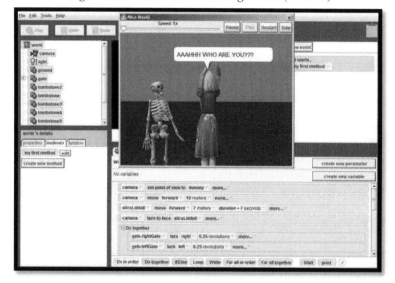

- **Model with mathematics**—*Translate scripts to your needs, not unlike decoding a formula in math. Figure 104a script (outlined in red) becomes Figure 104b picture:*

Figure 104a—The model; 104b—the result in Alice

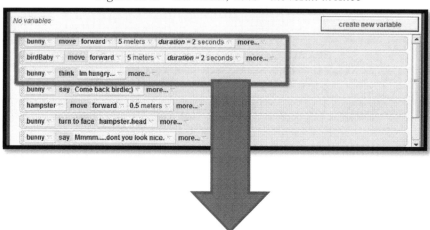

- **Use appropriate tools strategically**—*Alice does exactly what it is told, not what you wish it would. Be careful, logical and precise when programming (Figure 105):*

Figure 105—Use appropriate tools (Alice)

- **Attend to precision**—*to get the program to do what you want requires patience and precision. Demonstrating on the class screen is a good beginning (Figure 106a)*

Figure 106a—Attend to precision (in Alice); 106b—look for and express regularity

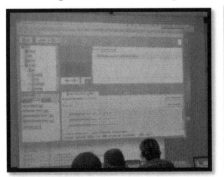

- **Look for and make use of structure**—*look at available tools and select those best suited for the task*

_____What is Alice: *A free programming game to teach basics to 8th grade and above without the intimidating techie-ness. With it, students create interactive stories, animations, and games.*

Figure 101a—Student using Alice; 101b—first world

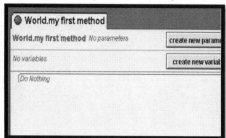

_____Besides Math Standards, Alice supports writing skills:

- *W.8.3a Engage and orient the Alice world viewer by establishing a context and point of view and introducing a narrator and/or characters; organize an event sequence that unfolds naturally and logically.*
- *W.8.3b Use narrative techniques in the Alice World, such as dialogue, pacing, description, and reflection, to develop experiences, events, and/or characters.*
- *W.8.3c In Alice world dialogue and action, use a variety of transitions to convey sequence, signal shifts from one time frame or setting to another, and show relationships among experiences and events.*
- *W.8.3d Use precision and appropriate tools throughout to convey events.*
- *W.8.3e Provide a conclusion to the Alice world story that follows events.*

_____This is a self-paced student-directed unit. Students work in groups.

_____Have groups go through tutorial by clicking "Start Tutorial" in *Welcome to Alice* dialogue box.

_____Done with tutorial? Create an animated avatar:

- Choose "room" template, then "Setup Scene."
- Choose "class Biped," "class Person," then child, female, light and avatar that is shown.
- Push OK until avatar appears in room.
- Using circle at avatar's feet, turn him/her until s/he faces right, then press "edit code."
- In tab that says, "this child/person," choose a body part and give it direction by moving instruction to method box. Run program to see results.
- Debug program if it doesn't work.

_____Stuck? Go through Alice online documentation, use Help files, and work with group mates. Do not give up. Do not get frustrated. Keep making changes. It will work.

Figure 107a-b—Alice programming

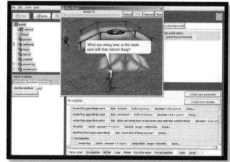

_____When you are comfortable in the Alice world, open a new Alice world and place a toy ball in the world. The goal: Make ball realistically roll. After sufficient time, articulate in your blog why this is harder than it sounds. What are suggestions for solving this?

- distance traveled by ball = circumference X number of revolutions toy ball makes
- algebraic equation is $t = \pi d \times v$, where t is distance traveled, πd is circle circumference, v is number of complete revolutions toy ball makes
- rewrite equation to be used in Alice, $v = t \div (\pi d)$
- use formula to make toy ball roll realistically

_____When students are comfortable in the Alice world, have them open a new Alice world and place a toy ball in the world. The goal: Make ball realistically roll. After sufficient time, ask separate groups to articulate why this is harder than it sounds:

- distance traveled by ball = circumference of circle X number of complete revolutions
- algebraic equation is $t = \pi d \times v$, where t is distance traveled, πd is circle circumference, v is number of complete revolutions toy ball makes
- rewrite equation to be used in Alice, $v = t \div (\pi d)$
- use this formula to make toy ball roll

Figure 108a-c—Math programming in Alice

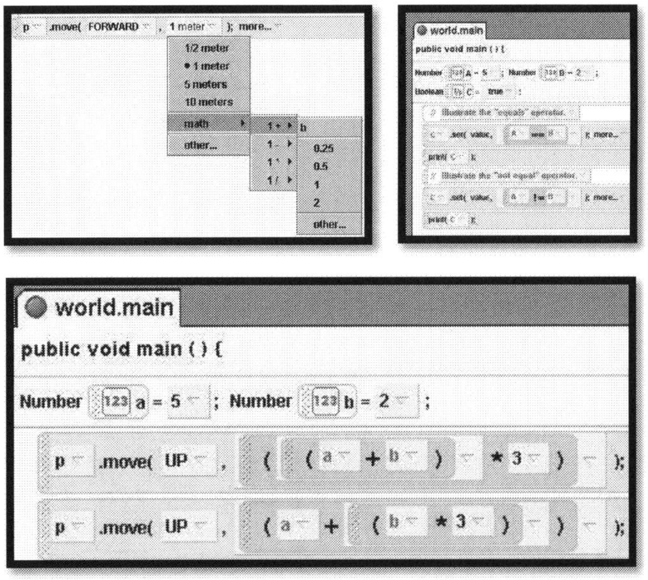

_____**Alternative task:** In groups, students watch movie trailer of *Despicable Me* (or similar). Analyze how avatars move limbs, mouths, and how they walk. As a class, compare to humans. For example, which leg moves first? How do joints move? How do arms and legs move in relation to each other? Does body bob up-down or side-to-side as avatar moves?

_____List movements and then construct a walking avatar in Alice world.

_____Students wrap up lesson by creating a rubric in a spreadsheet program (like Excel or Sheets). Include all requirements of the completed project. For example, if you were expected to include:

- *four objects*
- *good parameter/variable*

- *one event*
- *specific file name*
- *specific purpose for World*
- *specific method of reflecting on work*
- *specific way to share World*

...your rubric might look like *Figure 109*:

Figure 109—Alice rubric

Alice Project

Name		Teacher:	Date:	Class	
	4	3	2	1	
Objects	Has at least four objects in world.	Has three objects in world.	Has two objects in world.	Has one object in world.	
Parameter/ Variable	Has good use of parameter or variable in world.	Has a parameter or variable which is meaningless.	Has a parameter or variable but did not	Does not have any pararmeters or variables.	
Function	Has useful functions in world	Uses functions with little meaning	Function does not make sense.	No functions found in world.	
Events	Created an event and gave the user directions	Created an event and did not give user	Created an event that did not work.	Did not create an event.	
File Name	File was named the name of the project and your name.	Only had one of the requirements for naming; either your	Project was named randomly.	Project was not named.	
Purpose	World met the theme and had a purpose and audience in	World met the criteria but did not have an audience in mind.	World did not meet the criteria but had an audience in	World did not meet the criteria and did not have an	
Reflection	Refected on Blog with at least three sentences using propper grammer.	Reflected at least three sentences, but did not post on Blog, but were shared with teacher.	Reflections were less than three sentences and were not shared	Did not reflect.	
Sharing	Final Project was shared through Google Docs DropBox	Final Project was shared via jump drive.	Final Project was emailed.	Final Project was not shared with teacher.	

Class exit ticket: **None.**

Photos credit: Duke University
Image credit: Dick Baldwin

Differentiation

- *Have students create an animated object).*
- *Use Alice to create a PSA.*
- *Try Storytelling Alice with focus on 3D animated movies.*

Lesson #28-30 SketchUp

Vocabulary	Problem solving	Homework
• Arcs • Bounding edges • Component • Entity • Face • Icosahedron • Layer • Modeling • Offset • Path • Polygons • Primitives • Scale • Walk	• My screen froze (clear a dialogue box) • I'm stuck (think creatively, critically) • I don't understand (be an explorer and risk-taker) • Someone on my team doesn't like this program (help him/her) • I can't find the right tools (use shortkeys) • My text label won't move with my model (consider annotation tool instead of text) • I can't find the orbit, pan, zoom tools to move (try mouse wheel) • I want to explore my model at eye level (use Walk tool) • My computer froze (save early, often?)	Watch Sketch Up videos. Be prepared to discuss. Review notes; be familiar with Warehouse; know project you'd like to do Watch all videos; prepare reflections Keyboard 45 minutes, 15 minutes at a time
Academic Applications Art, Engineering, coding, STEM, STEAM	**Required Skills** Basic programming, curiosity, being a risk-taker	**Standards** CCSS: Math.Practice.MP NETS: 4a-b, 5c-d

Essential Question

How can games lead to learning?

Big Idea

Technology differentiates education in surprising ways

Teacher Preparation/Materials Required

- Insure SketchUp is loaded to all computers.
- Have traditional mouse, not track pad or track ball.
- Integrate domain-specific tech vocabulary into lesson.
- Have lesson materials online to preview lesson.
- Know whether you need extra time to complete lesson.
- Have student workbooks available (if using).
- Ask what tech problems students had difficulty with.
- Talk with grade-level team to tie into inquiry.
- Know which tasks weren't completed last week and whether they are necessary to move forward.
- Something happen you weren't prepared for? Show students how you fix the emergency without a meltdown and with a positive attitude.

Assessment Strategies

- Previewed required material; came to class prepared
- Used workbook to access links
- Completed SketchUp tasks
- Submitted reflection
- Used good keyboarding habits
- Completed warm-up
- Joined classroom conversations
- [tried to] solve own problems
- Decisions followed class rules
- Left room as s/he found it
- Higher order thinking: analysis, evaluation, synthesis
- Habits of mind observed

Steps

Time required: ***180 minutes or more***
Class warm-up: ***Keyboarding on the class typing program***

_____**Homework is assigned the week before this unit so students are prepared.** Expect students to review unit and come to class prepared.

_____Students have any tech problems they'd like help with? Keyboarding Questions?

_____Use backchannel program like Socrative to determine where you might offer assistance.

_____Unit is student directed. Expect them to learn by exploring and sharing knowledge.

_____Divide students into groups. Using these videos (if you don't find these on the internet, try Ask a Tech Teacher's resources pages for SketchUp):

- *Intro to SketchUp*
- *Getting Started with SketchUp—1-4*

...have each group select one video, discuss the following questions among themselves, and then present their thoughts to the class:

- *What is SketchUp and when/why is it used?*
- *How can it support math, science, history, or another academic subject?*
- *What class project (outside of tech class) might use SketchUp and why?*

_____If you'd like: Try these lesson series that walk students through SketchUp basics:

- this twenty-eight video Getting Started series (available from SketchUp)
- How-to SketchUp (available from Aidan Chopra website)

_____Open SketchUp. Students browse online documentation.

_____Introduce the SketchUp Warehouse. Browse to see what has been created (see *Figures 110a-c*).

Figure 110a-c—Designs from SketchUp Warehouse

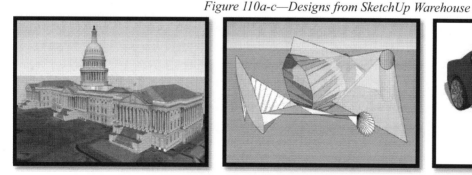

_____Next: In groups, create 3D geometric shapes like *Figures 111a-d* (SketchUp Warehouse):

Figure 111a-d—Geometric shapes in SketchUp

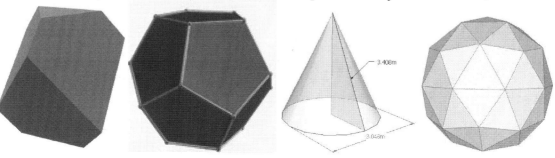

_____Next: In groups, create a building to scale (*Figure 112*):

Figure 112—House in SketchUp

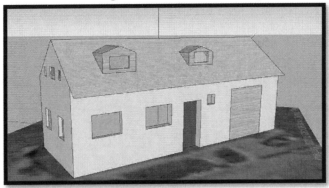

_____Start the house building by watching *Building a House in SketchUp* (on YouTube).
_____Next: Students will complete one of the following tasks that integrate SketchUp with math, geography, or science:

- *Find a SketchUp of a real building in the warehouse. Try to reproduce it. Then, compare your design to pros. In Figures 113a-b, which is real and which is SketchUp:*

Figure 113a-b: Which is real? Which is SketchUp?

- *Create an icosahedron (see 3DVinci on YouTube) like Fig. 114a.*
- *Design a building on your campus and upload to Google Earth (or Warehouse). Figure 114b is the Eliot School in St. Louis Missouri.*

Figure 114a—Icosahedron in SketchUp; 114b—building on campus

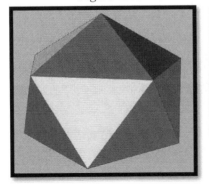 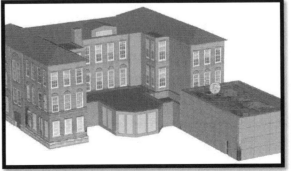

_____Once completed, submit project through class Dropbox, place a screenshot in a blog post with a reflection, and/or place a screenshot in a Tweet with a reflection

_____Knowing what you now know about SketchUp, where do you see it fitting into your educational landscape? A model of ancient Rome (*Figure 115a*)? Science (*Fig. 115b*)? Math (*Fig. 115c*)?

Figure 115a—Ancient Rome; 115b—molecules; 115c—math shapes

 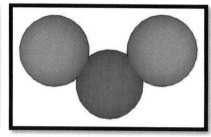 

_____All of these drawings are from the SketchUp 3D Warehouse.

Class exit ticket: **None.**

Differentiation

- Visit MathForum Sketchup pages.
- History: Create period furniture or buildings.
- Literacy: Create setting in a book—houses, buildings.
- Science: Build simple machines.
- Earth Science: Design volcanoes, horizon layers, plates.
- Instead of SketchUp, use 3DTin to model 3D objects.
- Have California 8th graders work with 4th graders and build California Mission in SketchUp.
- Take a picture from Google Earth and build SketchUp building from it.

Lesson #31-32 Web Communication Tools

Vocabulary	Problem solving	Homework
• Embed • GIF • Jing • Mindmap • Publish • Screencast • Screenshot • Scribd • Share • Widget	• I don't know how to embed a tool • Where's embed code? (search screen) • I see 'share' (click that) • I like the tool, but it charges a fee (look around for free version) • Login doesn't work (is it typed correctly?) • How do I save when there's no 'save' button? (try a screenshot) • I don't like the tool (try a different one) • I don't understand tool (ask teammates)	Be prepared to discuss three tools. Review notes to pre-pare for project Watch all videos; prepare reflections Keyboard 45 min., 15 minutes a time
Academic Applications research, collaboration, sharing, online safety	**Required Skills** Internet basics, use of online tools, inquiring mind, experience presenting to a group	**Standards** CCSS: SL.8.5 NETS: 1a-d, 3d, 7a-d

Essential Question

How do I use technology to differentiate communication?

Big Idea

Use technology to diversify and differentiate communication

Teacher Preparation/Materials Required

- Integrate domain-specific tech vocabulary into lesson.
- Know whether you need extra time to complete lesson.
- Have lesson materials and links online to preview.
- Work with grade-level teachers to support inquiry.
- Ask what tech problems students had difficulty with.
- Review what tools worked best last year.
- Test tools so you know which require log-ins or email.
- Know which tasks weren't completed last week.
- Something happen you weren't prepared for? Show students how you fix without a meltdown.

Assessment Strategies

- Previewed required material; came to class prepared
- Used good keyboarding habits
- Completed warm-up, exit ticket
- Completed project and rubric
- Followed agreed-upon rules for speaking and listening
- Joined classroom conversations
- [tried to] solve own problems
- Decisions followed class rules
- Left room as s/he found it
- Higher order thinking: analysis, evaluation, synthesis
- Habits of mind observed

Steps

Time required: **360 minutes or more**
Class warm-up: **Keyboarding on the class typing program**

_____Homework is assigned the week before this unit so students are prepared.

_____Any questions from homework? Expect students to review unit and come to class prepared.

_____For this project, groups select an online web communication tool from a list you provide (or they convince you is appropriate), teach themselves how to use it, and then teach classmates.

_____The list you provide should represent a variety of learning styles—textual, visual, auditory, art, music, and color. This is a great opportunity to differentiate instruction.

_____This Unit works best if students are working toward a final collaborative project that requires investigation and conclusions that they share and publish. Team up with grade-level teachers to identify such a topic.

_____If students use workbooks, they can quickly access webtools from their copies.

_____The goal is to broaden student exposure to available communication tools.

_____Many tools are intuitive, similar to what students already know, free, and require minimal log-in information.

_____Here's a sample list. Add your favorites:

- *Assessment Puzzles such as crosswords; Figures 116a-b:*

Figure 116a-b—Puzzle Maker

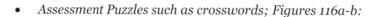

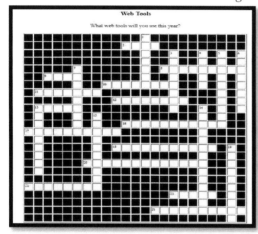

Across	Down
2. screencast	1. create videos with text and pictures
8. videos online	3. online posters
9. talking avatars	4. program in a 3D environment
10. create with text, website, more	5. Lots of learning visual tools
11. word clouds	6. curate collections of books
12. create a personalized map	7. online with links and more
13. visual timelines	13. polls and surveys
16. Lots of ways to format pictures	14. visual organizer templates
17. create and publishe slideshwos online	15. review with crosswords
18. tape studentsand share	19. collate lesson plan materials
20. tell a story with comics	
21. brainstorming	
22. prepare a quiz online	
23. create GIFs online	

- *BatchGeo—data entered into Figure 117a (intentionally blurred) gives you the map in Figure 117b:*

Figure 117a and 117b—BatchGeo

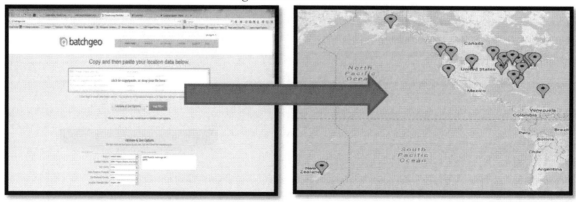

- *Code Monster—Figure 119:*

Figure 119b—Code Monster

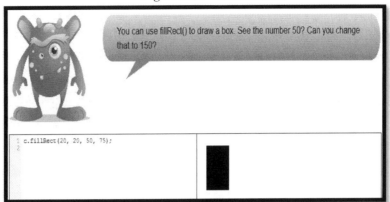

- *Comics (free)—use your favorite comic creator to tell a story; turn it into a video (Figures 120a-b):*

Figure 120a-b—Storytelling with comics

- *Diagrams Online from Gliffy Figure 121a*
- *GIMP—Figure 121b*

Figure 121a—Gliffy; 121b—GIMP

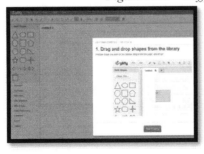 

- *an animated video program Figure 122:*

Figure 122—an animated video

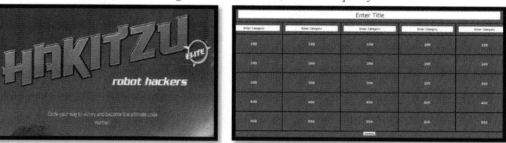

- *Hakitzu—Figure 123a*
- *Jeopardy Labs_– Figure 123b:*

Figure 123a—Hakitzu; 123b—Jeopardy

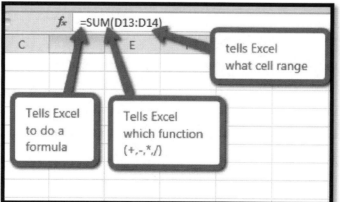

- *Your favorite screenshots/screencasts program; Figure 124a*
- *a favorite poll program like Google or Microsoft Forms— class polls; Figure 124b:*

Figure 124a—Screencast; 124b—Online Poll

- *Prezi Figure 125a:*

- *Online magazine Figure 125b:*

Figure 125a—Prezi; 125b—online magazine

- *Screencast-o-matic or your favorite screencast tool Figure 126a*
- *Haiku Deck or your favorite online presentation tool Figure 126b:*

Figure 126a—Screencast-o-matic; 126b—HaikuDeck

- *Stock Market Game Figure 127a*
- *Study Blue (or your favorite flashcard creator) Figure 127b:*

Figure 127a—Stock Market Game; 127b—Study Blue

 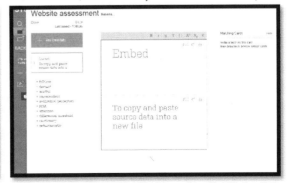

- *Canva -- create online fliers (Figure 128):*

Figure 128—Canva

- *Wolfram Alpha widgets — create a widget—Figure 129:*

Figure 129—Wolfram Alpha widget

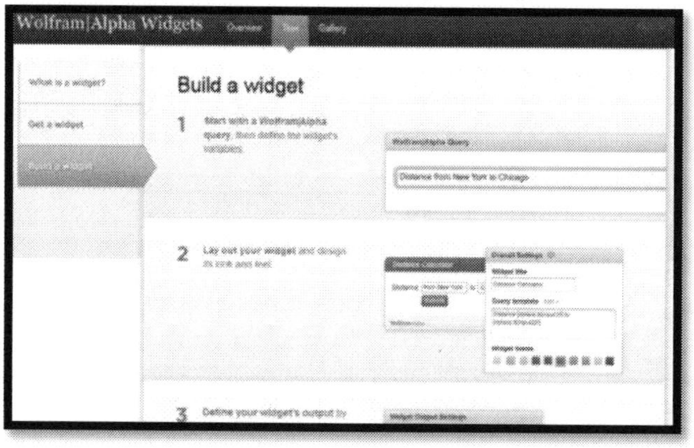

_____Review project grading in detail on class screen (see *Figure 130* and *Assessment* rubric at the end of the lesson). Explain each factor and take questions.

_____Have each group add their presentation date to class calendar.

_____Give students the rest of class to prepare. Presentations begin next week.

_____During presentation, one student will teach while others walk around and help classmates. The teacher will observe.

_____Follow appropriate rules of speaking and listening discussed in class:

- *Come to presentation prepared.*
- *Present information in a focused, coherent manner with relevant evidence, sound valid reasoning, and well-chosen details.*
- *Integrate multimedia to clarify, strengthen claims, and add interest.*
- *Pay attention to specific needs of this audience, this task, and this purpose.*
- *Use appropriate eye contact, adequate volume, and clear pronunciation.*

_____During presentation, students cover:

- *how to use tool*
- *how tool communicates ideas*
- *how to create a project*
- *how to troubleshoot*
- *how to embed project into blogs*
- *what students learned from the tool*

_____Audience will:

- *Be critical thinkers.*
- *Follow rules for collegial discussions displaying a respect for all opinions.*
- *Pose questions that connect ideas and/or respond to others' questions and comments.*

_____Each presentation will take about fifteen minutes. When the group is done, embed an example (or screenshot if an embed is not available) and directions for completing the project in their blog. Include a reflection on student experience.

Figure 8--Webtool assessment

Class exit ticket: **None.**

Differentiation

- *Upload projects to a class wiki page as a resource tool for other students interested in using these online tools.*

Assessment 21—Webtool Assessment

Webtool Assessment

Student names_____

Teacher name_____

CATEGORY	Exemplary—4 points	Developing—2 points	Unsatisfactory—0 points	RATING
Knowledge of selected tool **8 points**	Demonstrates clear understanding of how to use tool including terminology and tool website. Shows evidence of preparation for both group teaching and classmate problem-solving. Understanding is student-initiated with minimal assistance from teacher. Displays enthusiasm for tool and appreciation for its part in the learning experience. *When applicable, can show class how to embed completed tool into class blog. Knows which 'widget' to use and is able to help when classmates have difficulties.*	Demonstrates mixed understanding of tool. Shows some evidence of preparation for both teaching and problem-solving. Requires teacher assistance more than once. Displays some confidence in knowledge, enthusiasm for tool, and appreciation for its part in the learning experience. *Has some difficulty showing class how to embed completed tool into class blog or wiki page. Hasn't sufficiently prepared prior to teaching.*	Demonstrates a murky understanding of selected tool with little evidence of preparation for teaching or problem-solving. Requires substantial assistance from others to complete presentation. Displays lack of confidence in ability to make tool part in learning experience. *Unable to show class how to embed tool into class blog and/or wiki page.*	/8
Ability to teach students **4 points**	Demonstrates how to use tool in an authentic, personal, and enthusiastic manner. Uses terms class understands. Speaks slowly and clearly so class can complete steps. Provides trouble shooting and problem-solving tips (discovered as student learned to use tool).	Has some difficulty teaching students to use tool. Teaching lacks confidence and doesn't always engage students. Sometimes speaks too quickly for class to follow and some students are unable to complete project. Occasionally unable to trouble-shoot or problem-solve.	Has considerable difficulty teaching students. Teaching lacks confidence and doesn't engage students. Unable to trouble-shoot and problem-solve when asked. Students are unable to complete project.	/4
Reflection on tool's usefulness **4 points**	Reminds students how tool can be used to communicate the theme with examples. Fully addresses student questions about how to accomplish this. Reflection on blog is authentic and original, displays thoughtful analysis, and includes goals for continued learning.	Doesn't remind students of tool's usefulness but provides examples. Blog reflection shows insufficient original thought and incomplete itemization of goals for continued learning. Completed project not embedded as an example.	Reflection doesn't describe tool's use, shows little original thought, and does not include goals for continued learning. Blog includes inadequate reflection on usefulness of tool and no example of the tool itself.	/4
Group Work **4 points**	Consistently works toward group goals. Display sensitivity to feelings of others and values all members.	Sometimes works toward group goals. Is at times insensitive to the feelings of others.	Never works toward group goals or contributes. Is not sensitive to the feelings and needs of others in the group.	/4

PS

If you teach technology, it's likely you're a geek. Even if you didn't start out that way–say, you used to be a first grade teacher and suddenly your Admin in their infinite wisdom, moved you to the tech lab—you became a geek. You morphed into the go-to person for tech problems, computer quirks, crashes and freezes.

Overnight, your colleagues assumed you received an upload of data that allowed you to know the answers to their every techie question. It didn't matter that yesterday, you were one of them. Now, you are on a pedestal, their necks craned upward as they ask you: *How do I get the class screen to work?* Or: *We need the microphones working for a lesson I'm starting in three minutes. Can you please-please-please fix them?*

Celebrate your cheeky geekiness. Flaunt it for students and colleagues. Play Minecraft. That's you now–you are sharp, quick-thinking. You tingle when you see an iPad. You wear a flash drive like jewelry. The first thing you do when you get to school is check your email

It's OK. Here at Structured Learning and Ask a Tech Teacher, we understand. The readers understand. You're at home. To honor you, we've created these two posters (see next pages). They provide more ways to get your geek fully on as you go through your day.

Classroom Posters

1. 10 Steps to Become a Better Geek
2. 15 Ways to Get Your Geek On
3. Copyright Law
4. Digital Neighborhood
5. Email etiquette
6. Flipped Classroom
7. Here's What We've Done
8. How to Save—4 Ways
9. How to solve problems
10. I Can't Find My File
11. Keyboarding—why?
12. Netiquette Rules
13. Popular Shortkeys
14. Shortkeys—Chromebook
15. Shortkeys—Internet
16. Shortkeys—iPad
17. Shortkeys—PCs
18. Steps for Internet Research
19. What's a Mulligan

WHAT IS A...

Prepare for
class
the night before

FLIPPED CLASSROOM?

Apply learning to
class activitites

©AskATechTeacher

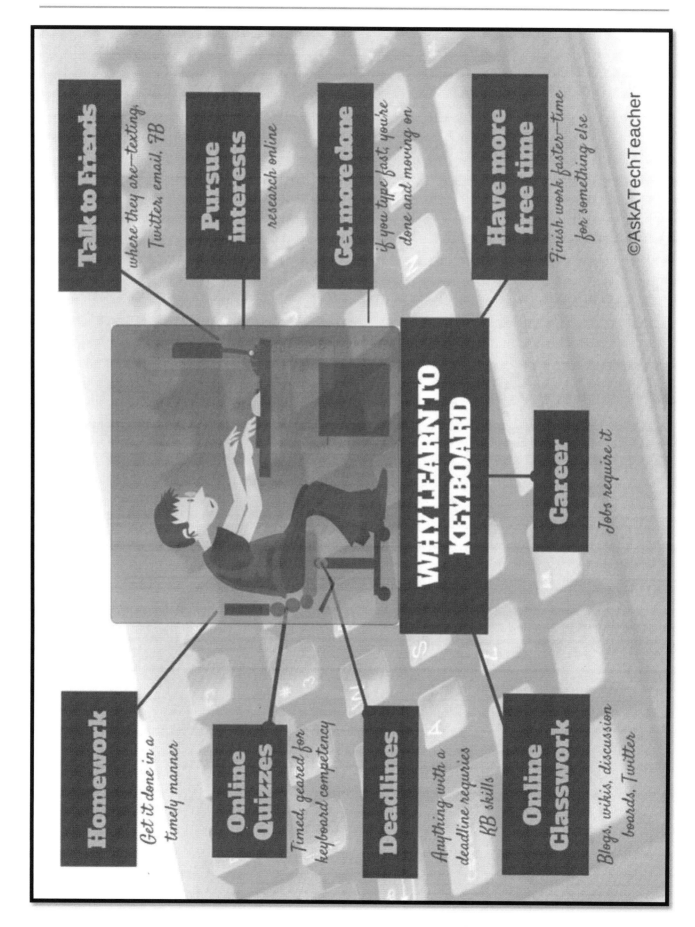

WHY LEARN TO KEYBOARD

Talk to Friends — where they are—texting, Twitter, email, FB

Pursue interests — research online

Get more done — if you type fast, you're done and moving on

Have more free time — Finish work faster—time for something else

Career — Jobs require it

Homework — Get it done in a timely manner

Online Quizzes — Timed, geared for keyboard competency

Deadlines — Anything with a deadline requires KB skills

Online Classwork — Blogs, wikis, discussion boards, Twitter

©AskATechTeacher

The law states that works of art created in the U.S. after January 1, 1978, are automatically protected by copyright once they are fixed in a tangible medium (like the internet) BUT a single copy may be used for scholarly research (even if that's a 2nd grade life cycle report) or in teaching or preparation to teach a class.

Don't talk to strangers. Look both ways before crossing the (virtual) street. Don't go places you don't know. Play fair. Pick carefully who you trust. Don't get distracted by bling. And sometimes, stop everything and take a nap.

©AskaTechTeacher

EMAIL ETIQUETTE

1. Use proper formatting, spelling, grammar
2. CC anyone you mention
3. Subject line is what your email discusses
4. Answer swiftly
5. Re-read email before sending
6. Don't use capitals—THIS IS SHOUTING
7. Don't leave out the subject line
8. Don't attach unnecessary files
9. Don't overuse high priority
10. Don't email confidential information
11. Don't email offensive remarks
12. Don't forward chain letters or spam
13. Don't open attachments from strangers

©AskaTechTeacher

Netiquette Rules
- Be human
- Follow the same rules of behavior you follow in real life
- Be aware of your digital footprint
- Share your knowledge
- Help keep 'flame wars' under control
- Respect other's privacy
- Be forgiving of other's mistakes

Popular shortkeys students love

Maximize window	**Double click title bar**
Quick Exit	**Alt+F4**
Date and Time	**Shift+Alt+D = Date**
	Shift+Alt+T = Time
Show taskbar	**WK (Windows key)**
Shows desktop	**WK+M**

Ctrl Key Combinations

- **CTRL+C: Copy**
- **CTRL+X: Cut**
- **CTRL+V: Paste**
- **CTRL+Z: Undo**
- **CTRL+B: Bold**
- **CTRL+U: Underline**
- **CTRL+I: Italic**

- **CTRL+P: Print**
- **CTRL+K: Add hyperlink**
- **CTRL+E: Center align**
- **CTRL+L: Left align**
- **CTRL+R: Right align**
- **CTRL+ : Zoom in Internet**
- **CTRL- : Zoom out Internet**

Fun Keyboard Shortcuts:

```
< + = + >  =  ⇔
— + >      =  →
:+)        =  ☺
```

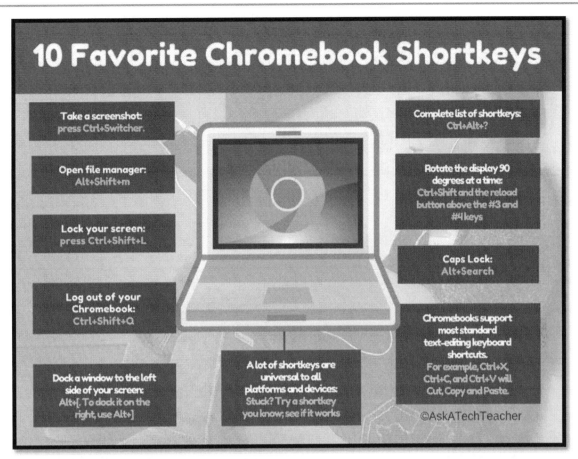

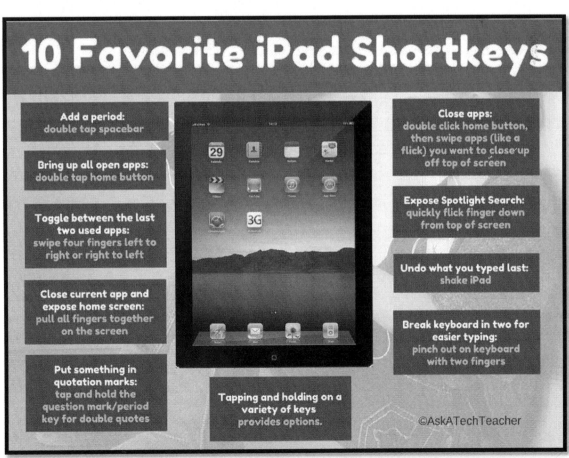

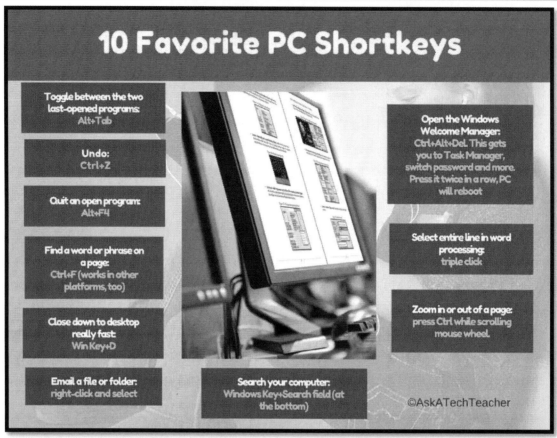

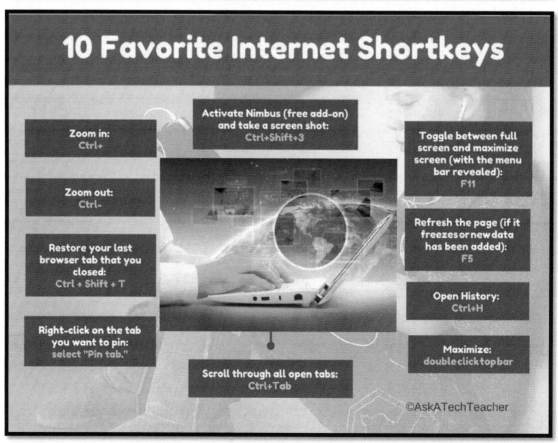

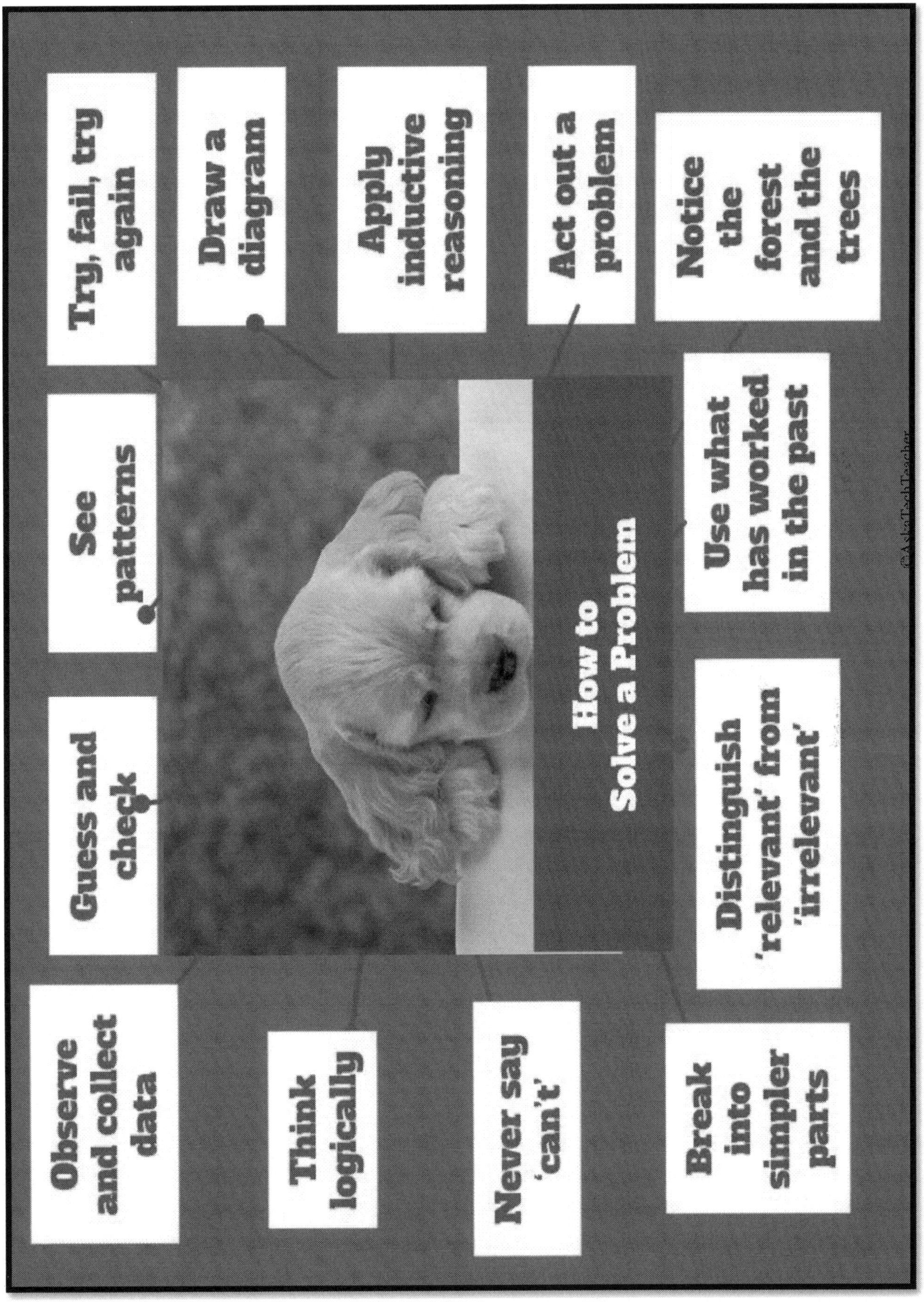

Try, fail, try again

Draw a diagram

Apply inductive reasoning

Act out a problem

Notice the forest and the trees

See patterns

Use what has worked in the past

Guess and check

How to Solve a Problem

Distinguish 'relevant' from 'irrelevant'

Observe and collect data

Think logically

Never say 'can't'

Break into simpler parts

STEPS FOR INTERNET RESEARCH

Know Key Words

General understanding of topic

Reliable site extensions

Read sidebars, headings, hyperlinks

Read pictures, insets, maps

GET YOUR DUCKS IN A ROW

©AskaTechTeacher

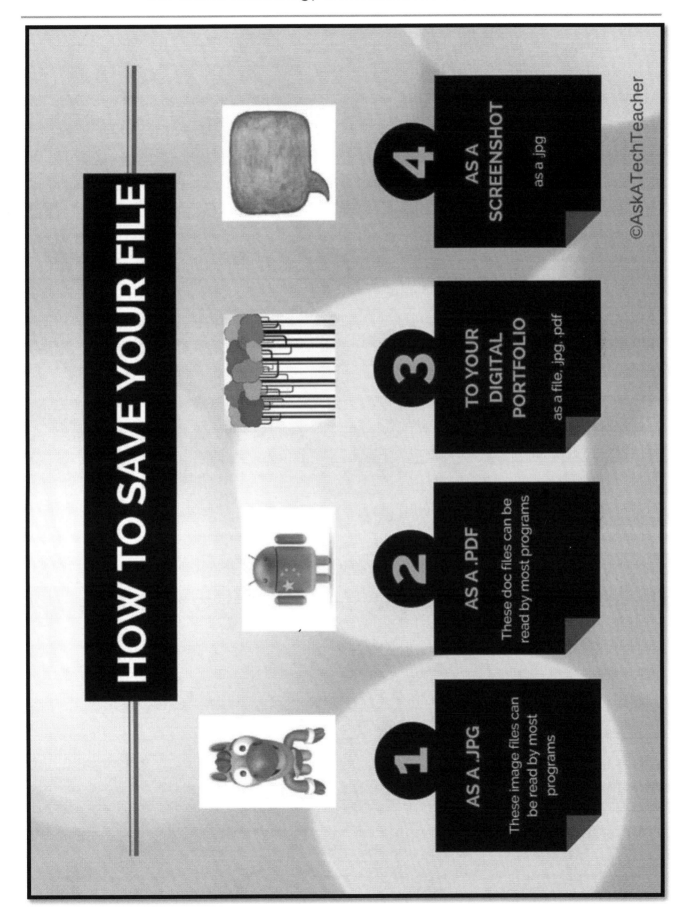

HOW TO SAVE YOUR FILE

1 AS A .JPG
These image files can be read by most programs

2 AS A .PDF
These doc files can be read by most programs

3 TO YOUR DIGITAL PORTFOLIO
as a file, jpg, pdf

4 AS A SCREENSHOT
as a jpg

©AskATechTeacher

What's a Mulligan?

1. Use **Tech**
2. Use **it** every day--save some trees
3. Use **it** when it seems difficult
4. Use **it** in class--and at home
5. Use **Tech** now--right now
6. Use **it** instead of something else
7. Teach a friend to use **it**
8. Teach a lot of friends to use **it**
9. Make **it** your first choice
10. Keep using **it**

15 ways To GET YOUR GEEK ON

1. Be smart. Yeah, it feels good
2. That's my inner Geek speaking
3. Think. Exercise your brain.
4. Waves. Sigh.
5. Keep repeating, *People are my friends*. Like Siri.
6. Move away from the keyboard--Not.
7. Some people watch TV. I play with a Rubik's Cube
8. Be patient. I'm buffering.
9. There must be a shortkey for that
10. Life needs an Undo key
11. Leave me alone for 2 minutes and I'll go to sleep
12. Yes, I can fix your computer
13. Like a computer, I do what you tell me to
14. My RAM is full. Come back later.
15. Slow down. My processor isn't that fast

Index

Certificate of Achievement

THIS ACKNOWLEDGES THAT

HAS COMPLETED THE HIGHLIGHTED 8TH GRADE TECHNOLOGY SKILLS:

- Digital citizenship
- Digital tools in the classroom
- Engineering and design
- Keyboarding, summative
- Learn through service
- Problem solving
- Programming with Alice

- Robotics
- SketchUp
- Spreadsheets
- Visual learning
- Web communication tools
- Search and research
- Word certification

Signatory

Signatory

Which book	Price (print/digital/Combo)
K-8th Tech Textbook (each)	$25.99-35.99 + p&h
K-8 Combo (all 9 textbooks)	$248-450 + p&h
K-8 Student workbooks (per grade—tech or kb)	$199/550/1500 (room/school/district)
35 K-6 Inquiry-based Projects	$31.99/25.99/52.18 + p&h
55 Tech Projects—Vol I,II, Combo	$18.99 /$35.38–digital only (free s&h)
K-8 Keyboard Curriculum—3 options	$20 and up + p&h
K-8 Digital Citizenship Curriculum	$29.95/25.99/50.38 + p&h
CCSS—Math, Language, Reading, Writing	$26.99 ea–digital only (free s&h)
K-5 Common Core Projects	$29.95/23.99/48.55 + p&h
Themed webinars	$8-30
Weekly tech webinars	Free or $99 per year for 180+ per year
Summer PD classes (online—for groups)	$795
Summer tech camp for kids	$179 + p&h
College credit classes (online)	$497 and up
Digital Citizenship certificate class	Starts at $29.99
Classroom tech poster bundles	Start at $9.99
PBL lessons--singles	$1.99 and up
Bundles of lesson plans	$4.99 and up (digital only)
Tech Ed Scope and Sequence (K-6 and 6-8)	$9.99 and up (digital only)
New Teacher Survival Kit	$285-620+ p&h
Homeschool Tech Survival Kit	$99 + p&h
Mentoring (30 min. at a time)	$50/session
169 Tech Tips From Classroom	$9.99 (digital only)
Consulting/seminars/webinars	Call or email for prices

Free sample? Visit Structured Learning LLC website
Prices subject to change
Email Zeke.rowe@structuredlearning.net

Pay via PayPal, Credit Card, Amazon, TPT, pre-approved school district PO

Structured Learning
Premiere Provider of Technology Teaching Books to the Education Community

Made in United States
Orlando, FL
10 August 2023

35958861R00120